Measurement

From the Read-Aloud Anthology

ONE INCH TALL

by Shel Silverstein

Access Prior Knowledge

This poem will help you review

- Addition and subtraction facts through 12
- Concept of length

ONE INCH TALL

If you were only one inch tall, you'd ride a worm to school.

The teardrop of a crying ant would be your swimming pool.

A crumb of cake would be a feast

And last you seven days at least,

A flea would be a frightening beast

If you were one inch tall.

If you were only one inch tall, you'd walk beneath the door,

And it would take about a month to get down to the store.

A bit of fluff would be your bed,

You'd swing upon a spider's thread,

And wear a thimble on your head

If you were one inch tall.

You'd surf across the kitchen sink upon a stick of gum.

You couldn't hug your mama, you'd just have to hug her thumb.

You'd run from people's feet in fright,

To move a pen would take all night,

(This poem took fourteen years to write—

'Cause I'm just one inch tall).

Name_____

Use the number line.
Solve.

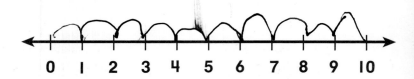

0 1 2 3 4 5 6 7 8 9 10

Draw or write to explain.

1. One worm is **6** inches long.
    Another worm is **4** inches long.
    They stretch along the number
    line end to end. How long are
    they altogether?

    ___**10**___ inches

2. A blue bird sees **4** worms.
    A red bird sees **6** worms.
    How many more worms does
    the red bird see?

    ___**2**___ more worms

3. A baby worm is **1** inch
    long. It grows **6** inches.
    How long is it now?

    ___**7**___ inches

4. Some worms are **2** inches
    long. A group of them stretch
    along a **10**-inch twig.
    How many worms are there?

    Skip count
    by 2s.

    ___**5**___ worms

5. **Talk About It** What would you do if you were
    one inch tall?

Dear Family,

My class is starting Unit 7. I will be learning about length and weight. I will also be learning about capacity and temperature. These two pages show what I will learn and have activities for us to do together.

From, _Moryan Brelage_

Vocabulary

These are some words I will use in this unit.

pound   A customary unit of weight

kilogram   A metric unit of mass

cup, pint, quart, liter   Units to measure capacity

thermometer   An instrument that measures how hot or cold something is

Some other words I will use are **measure**, **inches**, **centimeters**, and **weight**.

Vocabulary Activity

Let's work together to complete these sentences.

1. _pound_ and _Kilogram_ are used to measure how heavy an object is.

2. Capacity can be measured using _____ ,

   _____ , _____ , and _____ .

3. This instrument tells us how hot or cold something is. _____

> Turn the page for more.

How To measure objects with a ruler

In this unit I will be measuring objects. I will be using an inch ruler to measure length and height.

Measure

About how many inches long is the pencil?

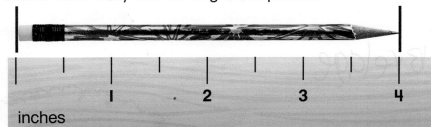

_____ inches

About how many inches long is the pencil?

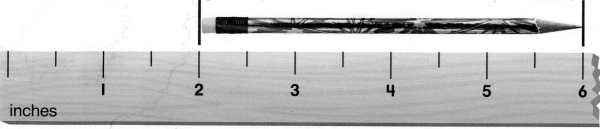

Count the spaces between the inch marks at both ends of the object.

_____ inches

Literature

These books link to the math in this unit. We can look for them at the library.

Inch by Inch
by Leo Lionni
(Bt Bound, 1999)

Measuring Penny
by Loreen Leedy

Lulu's Lemonade
by Barbara deRubertis

Let's read together!

Technology

We can visit *Education Place* at **eduplace.com/parents/mw/** for the Math Lingo game, *e* • Glossary, and more games and activities to do together.

Length and Weight

INVESTIGATION

In the picture find objects taller than a paper clip.

How Long Is It?

• • • • • • • • • • • • •

Use .

Find about how long the object is.

1.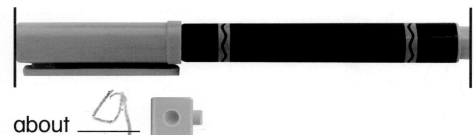

   about _____9_____

2.

   about _____13_____

3.

   about _____4_____

4.

   about _____0_____

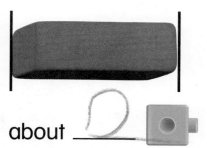

5. Which object is the longest? _____pencil_____

6. Which object is the shortest? _____eraser_____

Name_____

Activity: Compare and Order Length

Compare **length** and **height**.
Use **longer, taller, shorter**.

Objective
Compare and order length and height.
Vocabulary
length   longer
height   taller
            shorter

Step 1

Find the object.
Stand next to it.

The chair is shorter than you.

Step 2

Your partner tells if the object is shorter or taller than you.

Use **tall, taller, tallest** to compare three things.

 I am the tallest.

 I am taller.

I am tall.

Work Together

Is the object taller or shorter than you?
Circle.

1.

    taller

    (shorter)

2.

    taller

    shorter

3.

    taller

    shorter

4. **Talk About It** Which object above is the tallest?
   Which is the shortest?

Find the object.

Is the object longer or shorter than your hand?

Circle.

The book is longer than my hand.

1.    longer

   shorter

2.    longer

   shorter

3.    longer

   shorter

4.    longer

   shorter

Order your objects from shortest to longest.

Number the pictures.

The shortest object is 1.
The longest object is 4.

5.

   4   3   1   2

Color the longest pencil red.

Color the shortest pencil blue.

Draw a pencil that is longer than the red pencil.

6.

7. **Write About It** Is the red pencil still the longest? Why?

no Beca irdney4 longer one

At Home Have your child choose three kitchen objects, and then place them in order by length. Ask which is shortest and which is longest.

Name _____

Nonstandard Units

MathTracks 2/15
Listen and Understand

Objective
Estimate and measure length using nonstandard units.
Vocabulary
measure units

You can **measure** length with different **units.**

About how many 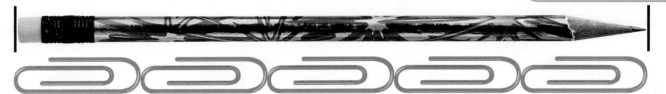 long is the pencil?

about ___5___ 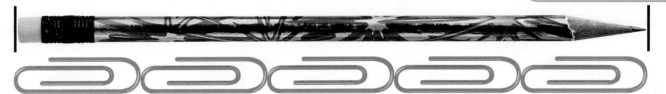 long

Line up the units. Make sure they touch end to end.

About how many 🔲 long is the pencil?

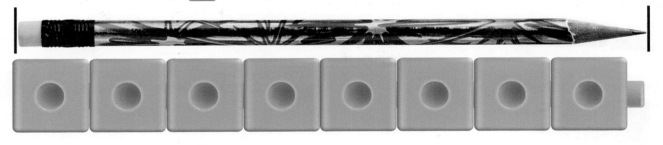

about ___8___ 🔲 long

Guided Practice

Complete the chart.

Find the object.	Measure with 📎.	Measure with 🔲.
1. 🖌	about _____ 📎	about _____ 🔲
2. 📓	about _____ 📎	about _____ 🔲
3. 🖍	about _____ 📎	about _____ 🔲

TEST TIPS **Explain Your Thinking** Can you mix cubes and paperclips when measuring an object? Why or why not?

Remember to line up the unit with the end of the object.

Choose a unit to measure the length.

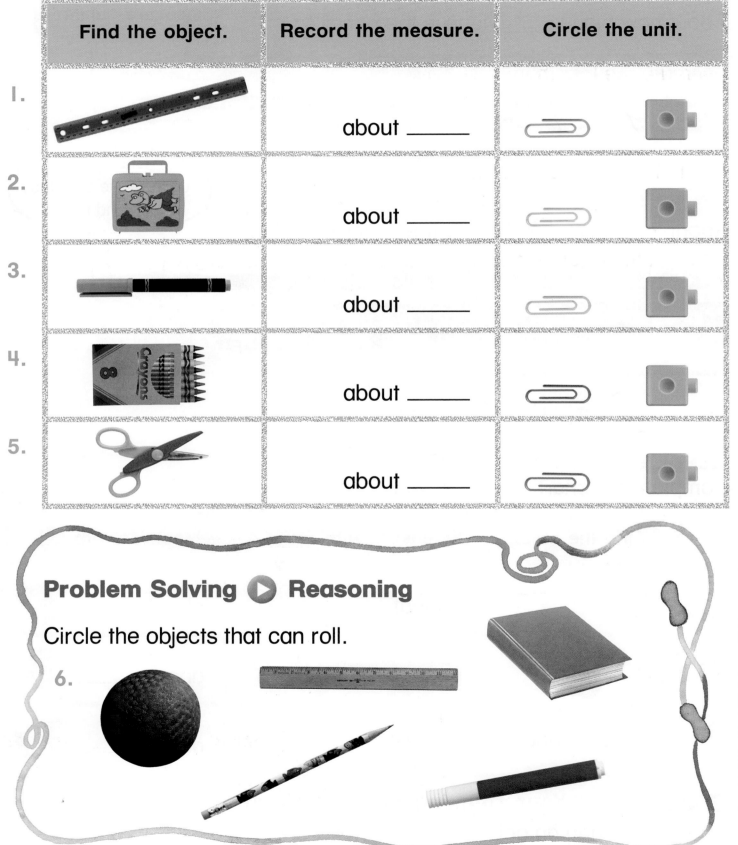

Find the object.	Record the measure.	Circle the unit.
1.	about _____	
2.	about _____	
3.	about _____	
4.	about _____	
5.	about _____	

Problem Solving ▶ Reasoning

Circle the objects that can roll.

6.

At Home Have your child use pennies as a unit to measure the length of objects at home.

Name_____

Activity: Inches

An inch is a unit of measure many people use.
You can estimate before you measure.

Hands-On

Objective
Estimate and measure an object in inches using a ruler.

Vocabulary
inches

Step 1

Estimate the length in **inches.**

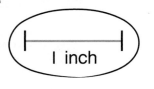
I inch

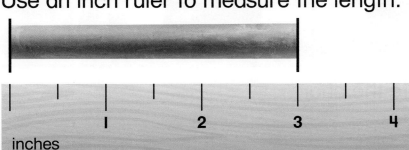

Estimate: about ___4___ inches

Step 2

Use an inch ruler to measure the length.

Line up the object with the end mark of the ruler.

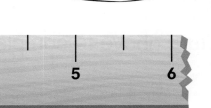

inches

Measure: about ___3___ inches

Work Together

Find the object.
Estimate.
Measure.

Think
Measure to the nearest inch.

1.

Estimate: about _____ inches   Measure: about _____ inches

2.

Estimate: about _____ inches   Measure: about _____ inches

Chapter 17 Lesson 3   five hundred three **503**

Remember to line up the object with the end mark on the ruler.

Use the picture above to complete the chart.

	1.	2.	3.	4.
Estimate	about ____ inches	about ____ inches	about ____ inch	about ____ inches
Measure	about 4 inches	about ____ inches	about ____ inch	about ____ inches

5. **Talk About It** Name three objects that are longer than 4 inches.

 At Home Ask your child to use an inch ruler to measure the length of objects such as spoons and forks.

Name_____

Centimeters

You can also measure length with **centimeters.**
Estimate the length.

I centimeter

Objective
Estimate and measure an object in centimeters using a ruler.
Vocabulary
centimeters

Estimate: about ___10___ centimeters

Use a centimeter ruler to measure the length.

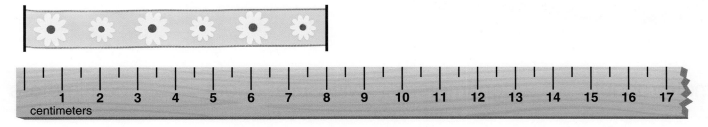

Measure: about ___8___ centimeters

Guided Practice

First estimate.
Then use a centimeter ruler to measure.

1.

Think
Look at the number where the ribbon ends.

Estimate: about _____ centimeters | Measure: about _____ centimeters

2.

Estimate: about _____ centimeters

Measure: about _____ centimeters

TEST TIPS **Explain Your Thinking** Name three objects that are shorter than 10 centimeters.

Remember to use the end marks to help you measure.

First estimate.
Then use a centimeter ruler to measure.

1.

Estimate: about _____ centimeters | Measure: about __17__ centimeters

2.

Estimate: about _____ centimeters | Measure: about _____ centimeters

3.

Estimate: about _____ centimeters | Measure: about _____ centimeters

4.

Estimate: about _____ centimeters

Measure: about _____ centimeters

Reading Math ▶ Vocabulary

5. Color the shortest feather ✏ .

6. Color the longest feather ✏ .

7. Circle the feather that is about **6** centimeters long.

At Home Ask your child to find objects at home that are longer than 10 centimeters. Then measure the objects.

Go on

Name_____

Measure Up

2 to 4 Players

What You Need: cubes, centimeter ruler, pencil, paper clip, and items on the spinner

How to Play

1. Take turns.
Spin the spinner.

2. Find that object.

3. Use a centimeter ruler to measure the object.

4. Take cubes to match the number of centimeters.

5. Group the cubes by 10s.
Play until one player has 50 cubes.

Other Ways to Play

A. Use an inch ruler.
Play until one player has 20 cubes.

B. Two players spin and measure. The player with the longest object scores 1 point. Play until one player has 5 points.

Quick Check

Find the object.
Is the object longer or shorter than your hand?
Circle.

1. 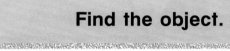 longer

shorter

2.  longer

shorter

Complete the chart.

3.

Find the object.	Measure with .
	about _____

First estimate.
Then use an inch ruler to measure.

4.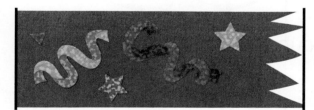

Estimate: about _____ inches

Measure: about _____ inches

First estimate.
Then use a centimeter ruler to measure.

5.

Estimate: about _____ centimeters

Measure: about _____ centimeters

Activity: Compare Weight

 MathTracks 2/16
Listen and Understand

You can compare the **weight** of objects.
Use a balance scale to find which is
heavier and which is **lighter.**

Objective
Compare and order the
weight of objects using
nonstandard units.

Vocabulary
weight
heavier
lighter

Step 1

Find two objects.
Estimate.
Which feels heavier?
Which feels lighter?

The book feels
much heavier than
the pencil.

Step 2

Put the objects
on a balance scale.
Compare the weight.

The side with the
book is lower.
The book is heavier.

Work Together

Find the object.
Circle the heavier object.

1.

2.

3.

4.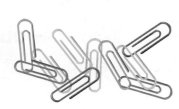

5. **Talk About It** Name three objects you could put in a
balance scale to use as units to measure weight.

Choose a unit to measure the weight.

Make both sides of the balance scale equal.

Find the object.	Record the measure.	Circle the unit.
6.	about _____	
7.	about _____	

Number the objects in order from lightest to heaviest.

The object that is the lightest is 1.

1.

_____   _____   _____

Circle the object that weighs about the same as two boxes.

2.

3. **Write About It** How do you know that two objects weigh about the same?

_____

_____

At Home Choose two kitchen objects. Ask your child which is heavier and which is lighter.

Name _____

Activity: Pounds

Objective
Compare and order the weight of objects.
Vocabulary
pounds

MathTracks 2/17
Listen and Understand

You can measure weight in **pounds.**

Step 1

Find the object.
Find a 1-pound weight.

less than 1 pound

Step 2

Weigh the objects on a balance scale.

about 1 pound

more than 1 pound

The juice is the heaviest object.
The soup is the lightest object.

Work Together

Compare the weight to 1 pound.
Circle.

Think
The side that is lower is more than 1 pound.

1.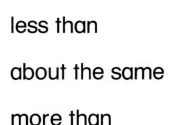

less than

about the same

more than

2.

less than

about the same

more than

3.

less than

about the same

more than

4. **Talk About It** Order the objects in Exercises 1–3 from lightest to heaviest.

Remember to think about objects you measured on the balance scale.

Circle.

Use  if the object weighs more than 1 pound.

Use  if the object weighs less than 1 pound.

1.

2. Pedro has these coins.
He buys a mask for 50¢.
How much money does
he have left?

_____¢

3. **Write About It** What coins could Pedro have left?

_____

At Home Have your child find three food items that weigh about 1 pound.

Activity: Kilograms

 MathTracks 2/18
Listen and Understand

You can measure how heavy an object is in **kilograms.**

Objective
Compare objects to a kilogram.
Vocabulary
kilograms

Step 1

Find the object.
Find an object that is 1 kilogram.

Step 2

Put the objects on a balance scale.

less than 1 kilogram

about 1 kilogram

more than 1 kilogram

Think
The side that is higher is the side that is less than.

Work Together

Compare the object to 1 kilogram.
Circle.

1.

less than

about the same

more than

2.

less than

about the same

more than

3.

less than

about the same

more than

4.

less than

about the same

more than

5. **Talk About It** Would you measure the length of a pencil in kilograms or centimeters? Why?

Remember to think about objects you measured on the balance scale.

Circle.

Use  if the object is more than 1 kilogram.

Use if the object is less than 1 kilogram.

1.

Write 9, 90, or 900 under each picture.

2.

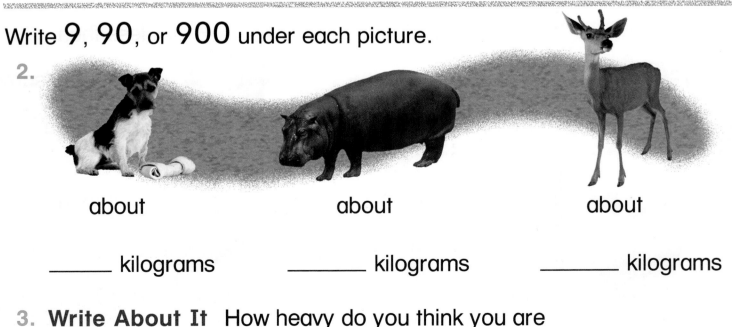

about

_____ kilograms

about

_____ kilograms

about

_____ kilograms

3. **Write About It** How heavy do you think you are

in kilograms? _____

At Home Help your child find three food items labeled in kilograms. Then compare them to find which is the heaviest and which is the lightest.

Name _____

Use Logical Reasoning

MathTracks 2/19
Listen and Understand

You can use clues to solve a problem.

Noelle wants a jump rope with handles.
She wants one shorter than the purple rope.
Which jump rope should she choose?

THINK ➡

DECIDE ➡

Noelle wants a jump rope with handles.	The green jump rope does not have handles. Cross out the green jump rope.
Noelle wants a jump rope shorter than the purple one.	She does not want the purple jump rope. Cross out the purple jump rope.
Which jump rope should Noelle choose?	Not the green. Not the purple. Noelle should choose the yellow jump rope. Circle the yellow jump rope.

The yellow jump rope makes sense.

It has handles. It is short.

Objective
Use logical reasoning to solve word problems.

Problem Solving

Guided Practice

Solve.

Circle the object that matches the clues.

1. It has squares on it. It is smaller than the orange ball.

> **Think**
> Cross out the ball with the dots.
> Find the one that is smaller than the orange ball.

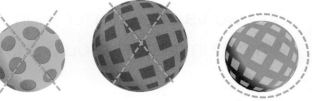

2. It is longer than the red bat. It is made out of metal.

> **Think**
> Cross out the red bat.
> Find the one that is metal.

Practice

3. It is blue. It is taller than the pink chalk.

4. It has handles. It is not the longest jump rope.

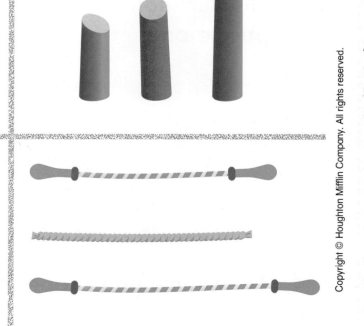

At Home Ask your child to explain how he or she used the clues to solve the problems.

Put the objects on a balance scale.
Circle the heavier object.

1.

2.

Circle.

Use  if the object weighs more than I pound.

Use if the object weighs less than I pound.

3.

Circle.

Use if the object is more than I kilogram.

Use if the object is less than I kilogram.

4.

Solve.

Circle the ball that matches the clues.

5. It has squares on it.
   It is larger than the
   ball with dots.

 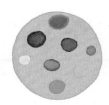 

Read the clock. Write the time.

1.

_____ o'clock

2.

half past _____

3.

_____ o'clock

4.

___ : ___

5.

___ : ___

6.

___ : ___

Social Studies Connection Growing Luca

Luca lives in Florida.
His parents measure him.
He is 48 inches tall.

Luca's aunt from Rome, Italy comes
to visit. His aunt measures him.
Luca is 122 centimeters tall.

Did Luca grow? What happened?

_____

_____

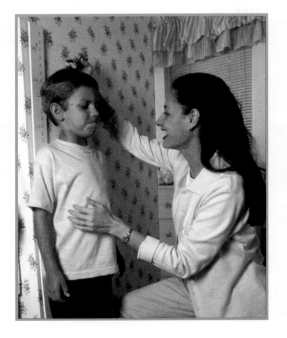

Vocabulary   *e* Glossary

Match the word to the correct statement.

1. **heavier**   a unit to measure length

2. **pound**   an object that weighs more

3. **centimeter**   a unit to measure weight

4. **height**   a measurement of how tall something is

Concepts and Skills

Find the object.

Is the object longer or shorter than your hand?

Circle.

5. 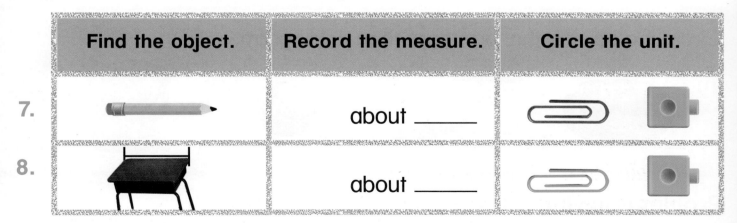   longer

                                    shorter

6.   longer

                                    shorter

Choose a unit to measure the length.

Find the object.	Record the measure.	Circle the unit.
7.	about _____	
8.	about _____	

First estimate.

Then use an inch ruler to measure.

9.    Estimate: about _____ inches

                                    Measure: about _____ inches

First estimate.

Then use a centimeter ruler to measure.

10.

Estimate: about _____ centimeters | Measure: about _____ centimeters

Circle the heavier object.

11.

12.

Circle the objects that weigh more than I pound.

13.

Circle the objects that are more than I kilogram.

14.

Problem Solving

Solve.

Circle the bat that matches the clues.

15. It is made out of wood.
    It is the shortest bat.

Capacity and Temperature

CHAPTER 18

INVESTIGATION

Find the object that can hold the most water.

PEOPLE USING MATH

Ben Franklin

Benjamin Franklin was an important person in our country in the 1700s. He was also a famous inventor who enjoyed music. Franklin once saw musical glasses filled with water. Different tunes were played on them. He invented an instrument called the armonica. Sounds are created on the instrument by rubbing water on different shaped glasses.

Ben Franklin playing his armonica.

You Can Make Your Own Musical Glasses

The amount of water and thickness of the glasses can change the tune. Songs like "Twinkle, Twinkle, Little Star," "The Itsy, Bitsy Spider," or "I'm a Little Tea Pot" can be played on the glasses.

Name_____

Activity: Cups, Pints, and Quarts

 MathTracks 2/20
Listen and Understand

Use **cups**, **pints**, and **quarts** to tell
how much a container holds.

2 cups = 1 pint   2 pints = 1 quart

Step 1

Fill the smaller container.
Pour it into the larger container.

Step 2

Continue until the larger
container is full.

Work Together

Use cups, pints, and quarts.
Complete the table.

Count as you pour
each container.

How many?	Number
1. cups in a pint	_____ cups
2. pints in a quart	_____ pints
3. cups in a quart	_____ cups

4. **Talk About It** How many cups of milk fill a
1-quart container? How do you know?

Use cups, pints, and quarts to compare.
Circle which holds more.

1.

2.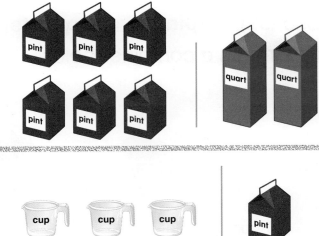

3.

4.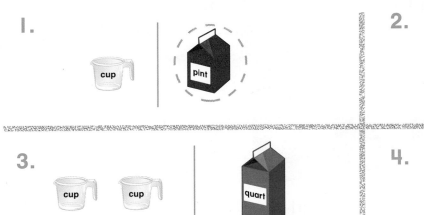

Circle which can hold the same amount.

5.

6.

7. How many more cups does the vase hold than the mug?

_____ more cups

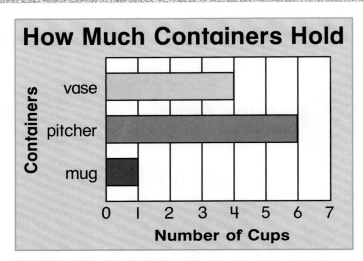

How Much Containers Hold

8. **Talk About It** Create a question you can answer by using the graph.

At Home Ask your child to find containers at home that can hold 1 cup, 1 pint, and 1 quart.

Name_____

Activity: Liters

MathTracks 2/21
Listen and Understand

You can also use **liters** to tell how much a container can hold.

Objective
Compare and order the capacity of containers to a liter.
Vocabulary
liters

Step 1

Fill a liter bottle.
Find the container.

The vase is not full. So, the vase can hold more than 1 liter.

Step 2

Pour the liter bottle into the container.

less than 1 liter   1 liter   more than 1 liter

Work Together

Compare to 1 liter.
Circle.

Think
Does the liter bottle fill the vase?

1.
less than
about the same
more than

2.
less than
about the same
more than

3.
less than
about the same
more than

4.
less than
about the same
more than

5. **Talk About It** Would you use a liter container to fill a swimming pool? Why?

Circle.

Use  if the object can hold more than I liter.

Use if the object can hold less than I liter.

1.

Circle the containers that can hold more than I liter.

2.

Remember this is I liter.

Go on

Name_____

Number the objects.

1 holds the least amount.

3 holds the greatest amount.

3.
_____1_____
_____3_____
_____2_____

4.
_____
_____
_____

5.
_____
_____
_____

Underline the words that tell how much a container can hold.

Circle the words that tell how long an object is.

6. cup   7. liter

8. centimeter   9. quart

10. pint   11. inch

12. **Write About It** What other containers can hold more than **1** liter? _____

Quick Check

Number the objects.

1 holds the least amount.

3 holds the greatest amount.

1.

_____   _____   _____

Circle which can hold the same amount.

2.

3.

Circle the objects that can hold more than **1** liter.

4.

Circle the objects that can hold less than **1** liter.

5.

Name _____

Temperature

You can use the words **hot** and **cold** to describe the **temperature.**

Use a **thermometer** to measure temperature.

The temperature is **90 degrees.**

90 degrees is hot.

The temperature is **30** degrees.

30 degrees is cold.

Guided Practice

Circle **hot** or **cold** to tell about the temperature.

1. 20 degrees

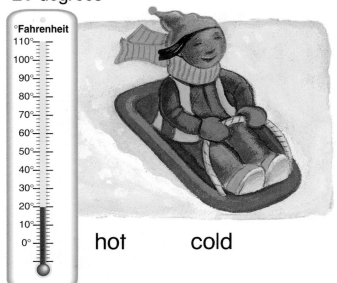

hot   cold

2. 85 degrees

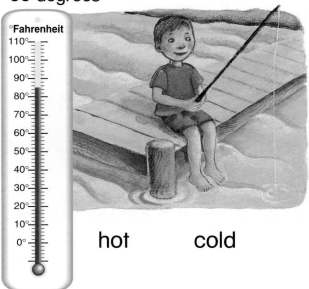

hot   cold

TEST TIPS **Explain Your Thinking** Look at the temperatures. Which is the hottest? Which is the coldest?

Circle **hot** or **cold** to tell about the temperature.

1. 10 degrees

hot ⬭cold⬭

2. 80 degrees

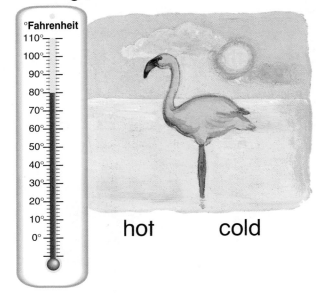

hot   cold

3. 100 degrees

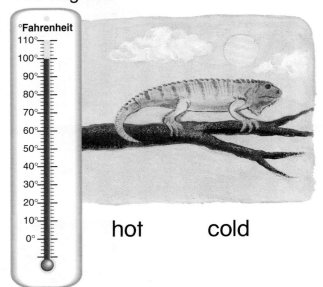

hot   cold

4. 25 degrees

hot   cold

Problem Solving ▶ Reasoning

Order the pictures **1**, **2**, and **3**.
Write **1** for the coldest. Write **3** for the hottest.

5. 55 degrees    30 degrees   🍝 90 degrees

_____   _____   _____

🏠 **At Home** Ask your child to identify familiar foods as **hot** or **cold**.

Name_____

Reasonable Answers

Choose the answer that makes more sense.

Dawn makes a terrarium. She puts
pebbles, soil, and plants into a bowl.
She needs to find out if a tall
plant will fit.

**What should she use to measure
the height of the plant?**

Objective
Choose the more
reasonable measuring
tool to solve problems.

THINK

DECIDE

Dawn needs to measure the height of the plant.	She needs to choose a measuring tool.
A ruler measures length or height.	She needs to measure the height of the plant.
A balance scale measures how heavy something is.	She does not need to know how heavy the plant is.
Which tool should Dawn use?	The ruler. It measures height.

**The ruler is the more reasonable answer.
It makes more sense.**

Circle the answer that makes more sense.

1. Jimmy wants to know how long the side of the fish tank is. What can he use to find out?

   Think
   Which measures how long something is?

2. Tyler wants to know how much water is in his fish tank. What can he use to find out?

   Think
   Which measures how much something holds?

3. Maia has a stone and a rock. What can she use to find out which is heavier?

4. Pete needs to know the temperature of the water in his fish tank. What can he use to measure?

At Home Ask your child to tell why the answers he or she chose are reasonable and why the others do not make sense.

Name_____

Circle **hot** or **cold** to tell about the temperature.

1. 15 degrees

hot   cold

2. 90 degrees

hot   cold

3. 30 degrees

hot   cold

4. 85 degrees

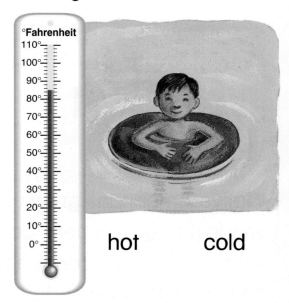

hot   cold

Circle the answer that makes more sense.

5. Hector wants to know how long his string is. What can he use to find out?

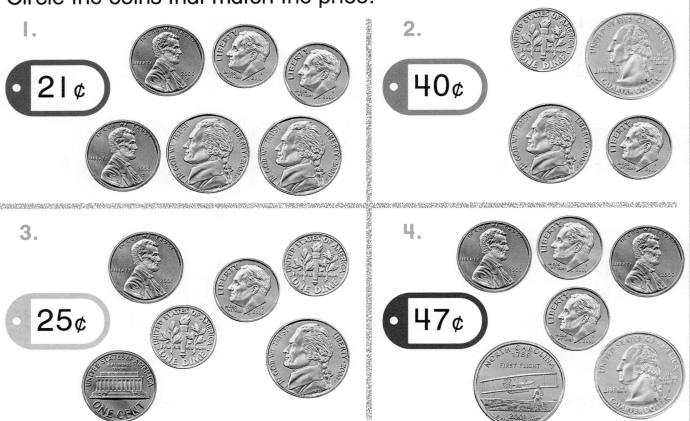

Key Topic Review

Circle the coins that match the price.

1. 21¢

2. 40¢

3. 25¢

4. 47¢

Social Studies Connection

Johnnycakes

Native Americans grew corn and made it into cornmeal. Johnnycakes were made from cornmeal. They are like pancakes and could be taken on long trips, or journeys.

Pioneers called them "journey cakes" or johnnycakes.

1 cup of cornmeal makes johnnycakes for 4 people. How many cups of cornmeal do you need for 8 people?

_____ cups

WEEKLY WR READER eduplace.com/kids/mw/

Name_____

Vocabulary *e* Glossary

| cups | liters | thermometer |

Complete the sentence.

1. There are 2 _____ in a pint.

2. A _____ tells you how hot or cold something is.

3. You can use _____ to tell how much a container holds.

Concepts and Skills

Circle the container that can hold more.

4.

5.

Number the objects.
1 holds the least amount.
3 holds the greatest amount.

6.

_____   _____   _____

Circle which holds more.

7. |

8.  |

Chapter Review / Test

Circle which can hold the same amount.

9. | |

10.  | |

Circle.

Use  if the object can hold more than 1 liter.

Use  if the object can hold less than 1 liter.

11.

Circle **hot** or **cold** to tell about the temperature.

12. 20 degrees

hot   cold

13. 80 degrees

hot   cold

14. 40 degrees

hot   cold

Problem Solving

Circle the answer that makes more sense.

15. Megan wants to know if she needs to wear a jacket outside. What should she use to find out?

 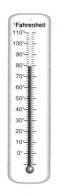

Name_____

Add.
Write the sum.

1.	5 +7	2 +9	5 +5	8 +1	1 +3	5 +3	3 +6

2.	5 +2	7 +1	9 +0	6 +4	3 +3	1 +4	7 +4

3.	2 +6	7 +3	4 +2	3 +4	7 +2	6 +6	3 +7

4.	6 +4	3 +5	8 +0	0 +0	1 +5	9 +2	3 +5

5.	3 +9	6 +5	2 +7	9 +1	0 +6	3 +8	1 +1

6.	4 +8	2 +5	0 +1	2 +3	9 +3	3 +2	2 +2

7.	2 +4	4 +0	8 +3	6 +2	4 +7	4 +5	8 +4

Facts Practice

Subtract.
Write the difference.

1.
$$12 - 5$$ $$10 - 2$$ $$7 - 1$$ $$10 - 7$$ $$9 - 4$$ $$7 - 5$$ $$11 - 4$$

2.
$$9 - 9$$ $$11 - 2$$ $$10 - 5$$ $$5 - 4$$ $$12 - 4$$ $$10 - 8$$ $$9 - 3$$

3.
$$11 - 7$$ $$12 - 3$$ $$10 - 9$$ $$6 - 2$$ $$4 - 4$$ $$10 - 3$$ $$9 - 2$$

4.
$$12 - 8$$ $$7 - 6$$ $$8 - 3$$ $$12 - 7$$ $$9 - 6$$ $$6 - 4$$ $$11 - 5$$

5.
$$11 - 6$$ $$2 - 0$$ $$12 - 6$$ $$7 - 2$$ $$8 - 1$$ $$10 - 4$$ $$12 - 8$$

6.
$$12 - 4$$ $$9 - 5$$ $$11 - 9$$ $$5 - 3$$ $$7 - 4$$ $$8 - 2$$ $$6 - 5$$

7.
$$12 - 3$$ $$4 - 3$$ $$7 - 3$$ $$11 - 5$$ $$8 - 4$$ $$6 - 3$$ $$12 - 7$$

Dolphins

Marc and his class visit the Dolphin Research Center in Florida. They learn that dolphins are very smart animals. Some dolphins are learning the difference between **more** and **less**.

The children also learn the names of some of the dolphins, like Pandora, Pax, Talon, and A.J.

Use an inch ruler to measure. Solve.

Draw or write to explain.

1. How long is the picture of the dolphin?

about _____ inches

2. The pictures are not the same length. Whose picture is longer?

Talon

Pax

_____

Dolphin	Pounds of Fish
Pandora	9
A.J.	12
Pax	11
Talon	20

Dolphins eat fish every day. This is how much fish each dolphin eats in one day.

Solve.

Draw or write to explain.

1. A.J. and Pandora are eating together. How many more pounds of fish does A.J. eat than Pandora?

_____ more pounds of fish

2. Which dolphin eats the most pounds of fish?

_____

Circle.

3. In the morning Pax eats fewer pounds of fish than Talon. Which bucket holds fewer pounds of fish?

 Technology
Visit *Education Place* at **eduplace.com/kids/mw/** to learn more about this topic.

Vocabulary e · Glossary

Match the word to the correct statement.

1. **inch**   a measure of how heavy an object is

2. **weight**   a unit to measure temperature

3. **degree**   a unit to measure length

4. **pound**   a unit to measure weight

Concepts and Skills

First estimate.
Then use an inch ruler to measure.

5.

Estimate: about _____ inches   Measure: about _____ inches

First estimate.
Then use a centimeter ruler to measure.

6.

Estimate: about _____ centimeters   Measure: about _____ centimeters

Circle the heavier object.

7.    8.

Circle the objects that weigh more than **1** pound.

9.

Circle the objects that are more than **1** kilogram.

10.

Circle which holds more.

11. cup cup  cup | quart

12.  pint pint |  quart quart

Circle **hot** or **cold** to tell about the temperature.

13. 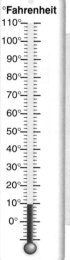 10 degrees

hot   cold

14.  90 degrees

hot   cold

Problem Solving

Circle the answer that makes more sense.

15. Christos wants to measure milk to make a cake. Which tool should he use?

   cup

1. Draw a fish that is about 2 inches long.
   Draw a turtle that is about 15 centimeters long.
   Draw a worm that is shorter than the fish.

   Which animal is the longest?

   Show your work using pictures, numbers, or words.

   _____

2. Draw a picture of something that weighs less than 1 pound.

   Show your work using pictures, numbers, or words.

Solve.

3. Jack finds this bird feather.
He wants to know how long it is.
What can he use to find out?

Draw a picture of the tool he can use.
Write the name of the tool.

Show your work using pictures, numbers, or words.

_____

Using a Ruler

Use an inch ruler to measure.

1.

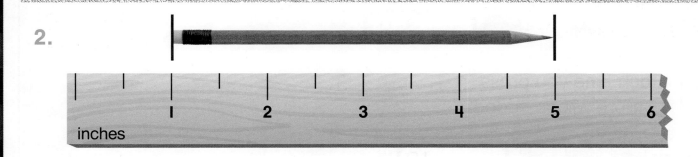

Measure: about ___2___ inches

2.

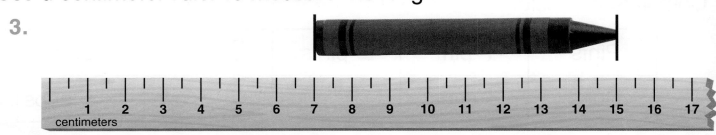

Measure: about _____ inches

Use a centimeter ruler to measure the length.

3.

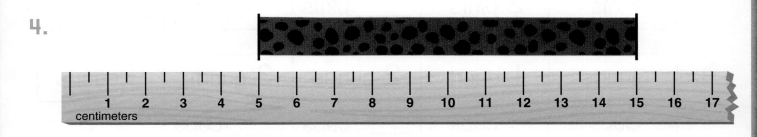

Measure: about _____ centimeters

4.

Measure: about _____ centimeters

⊙ **Technology**
Visit *Education Place* at
eduplace.com/kids/mw/ for brain teasers.

Technology Time

Calculator
Fill It Up!

There are **2** pints in **1** quart.
How many pints are in **5** quarts?

Use a .

Find the number of pints in **5** quarts.

Press: **2** **+** **2** **=** 4

Each time you press **=** ,
2 more will be added.

Press: **=** **=** **=** 10

_____ pints

Use a .
Complete the table.

1.

Pints	1 pint	2 pints	3 pints	4 pints
Cups	2 cups	_____ cups	_____ cups	_____ cups

2.

Quarts	1 quart	2 quarts	3 quarts	4 quarts
Pints	2 pints	_____ pints	_____ pints	_____ pints

3.

Quarts	1 quart	2 quarts	3 quarts	4 quarts
Cups	4 cups	_____ cups	_____ cups	_____ cups

Explain Your Thinking Which is greater, **6** cups or
4 pints? Why?

Name_____

Test-Taking Tips
• •

Make a drawing to help solve a problem.

Narrow the choices by quickly finding the ones that cannot be correct.

Multiple Choice

Fill in the ○ for the correct answer.

1. About how long is the feather?

I inch   3 inches
  ○   ○

6 inches   10 inches
  ○   ○

2. Which of these weighs about
    1 pound?

○   ○   ○   ○

3. What is the missing addend?

$$7 + \boxed{} = 12$$

2   3   4   5
○   ○   ○   ○

4. What comes next in
    this pattern?

○○○□△○○□△○

○   ○   ○   ○

Multiple Choice

Fill in the ○ for the correct answer. NH means Not Here.

5. Which equals 1 quart?

○

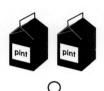
○

6. Which container holds more than 1 liter?

 ○    ○   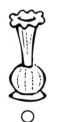 ○

7. The temperature is 25 degrees. What should Dara wear when she goes outside?

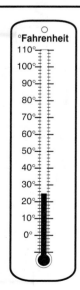

○   ○   ○   NH
○

Open Response

Solve.

8. Anton needs 3 pints of milk in a recipe. He only has a 1-cup measure. How many cups of milk does he need?

_____ cups

9. The Garcia family makes 12 tacos. They eat 9. Then they make 2 more. How many tacos do they have now?

_____ tacos

10. How much is there in all?

_____ ¢

 Test Prep on the Net
Visit *Education Place* at
eduplace.com/kids/mw/
for more test prep practice.

Two-Digit Addition and Subtraction

From the Read-Aloud Anthology

one watermelon seed

story by Celia Barker Lottridge • pictures by Karen Patkau

Access Prior Knowledge

This story will help you review

• Counting by tens

• Tens and ones

Max and Josephine planted a garden.

The rain fell and the sun shone. The seeds and the leaves, the stalks and the vines grew and grew and grew.

Max and Josephine weeded and watered and waited. One day they looked at their garden and saw there was plenty to pick. So . . .

Max picked thirty eggplants, dark and purple,
and forty peppers, shiny yellow.

Name_____

Use the picture on page 551a.
Count and add the vegetables.

Remember to start with the greater number and count on.

1.

+ ☐ peppers
☐ corn stalks
_____
☐ peppers and corn stalks in all

2.

+ ☐ eggplants
☐ peppers
_____
☐ eggplants and peppers in all

Use the pictures on pages 551b and 551c.
Solve.

3. 10 eggplants fit in a basket. Max fills 2 baskets. Then he collects 10 more eggplants. How many eggplants does he collect altogether?

Draw or write to explain.

_____ eggplants

4. Josephine picks 10 more eggplants than Max. How many eggplants does she pick in all?

_____ eggplants

Dear Family,

My class is starting Unit 8. I will be learning about adding and subtracting two-digit numbers. These two pages show what I will learn and have activities for us to do together.

From, _____

Vocabulary

These are some words I will use in this unit.

double   A basic fact that adds the same two numbers, like $3 + 3 = 6$, $5 + 5 = 10$, and $8 + 8 = 16$

tens   In the number 80, there are 8 tens.

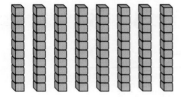

difference   The answer to a subtraction problem

In the problem $60 - 20 = 40$, 40 is the difference.

Vocabulary Activity

Let's work together to complete these sentences.

1. A fact like $4 + 4 = 8$ is a _____ fact.

2. If you have **50** tomatoes and you sell **30**, then **20** are left.

   The number **20** is called the _____ .

Turn the page for more.

How To subtract two-digit numbers

This two-digit subtraction problem is an example of what I will be learning. Sometimes I will use tens and ones blocks to help me find the answer.

Find 38 − 15.

Step 1	Step 2	Step 3
Show 38.	Subtract the ones.	Subtract the tens.

Step 1

Workmat 5

Tens	Ones

Tens	Ones
3	8
− 1	5

Step 2

Workmat 5

Tens	Ones

Tens	Ones
3	8
− 1	5
	3

Step 3

Workmat 5

Tens	Ones

Tens	Ones
3	8
− 1	5
2	3

Literature

These books link to the math in this unit. We can look for them at the library.

Counting Cranes
by Mary Beth Owens

Dinner at the Panda Palace
by Stephanie Calmenson
Illustrated by Nadine Bernard Westcott
(Bt Bound, 1999)

Lights Out!
by Lucille Recht Penner

Let's read together!

Technology

We can visit *Education Place* at **eduplace.com/parents/mw/** for the Math Lingo game, *e* • Glossary, and more games and activities to do together.

Addition Facts Through 20

INVESTIGATION

Count how many plants there are altogether.

How Does Your Garden Grow?

Listen to your teacher.

Show each story with .

Complete the number sentence.

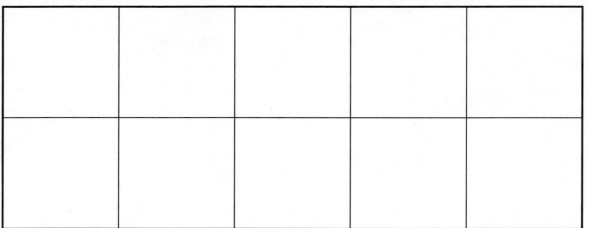

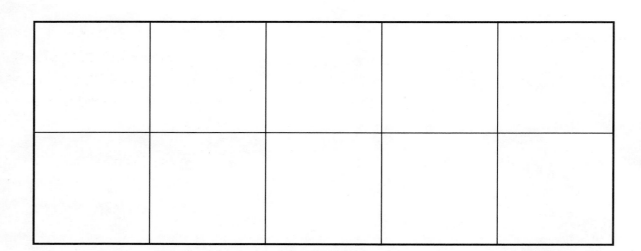

1. _____  + _____  = _____

2. _____  + _____  = _____

Name_____

Doubles Plus One

A **double** fact has two addends that are the same.

6 + 6 = __12__

Use the double fact to help you find other sums.

6 + 7	7 + 6
Draw 1 more.	Draw 1 more.

Find the sum.	Find the sum.
6 + 7 = __13__	7 + 6 = __13__

Guided Practice

Use the double fact.
Draw 1 more. Find the sum.

> **Think**
> I know the sum of 8 + 8.
> I draw 1 more to find
> 8 + 9 and 9 + 8.

1. 8 + 8 = _____

8 + 9 = _____   9 + 8 = _____

2. 7 + 7 = _____

7 + 8 = _____   8 + 7 = _____

TEST TIPS **Explain Your Thinking** How can you use a double fact to find the sum of 5 + 6?

Use a double fact
and add 1 more.

Find the sum.

1. ●●●●●
○○○○○

$5 + 5 = \underline{10}$

●●●●●●
○○○○○

$6 + 5 = \underline{11}$

●●●●●
○○○○○○

$5 + 6 = \underline{11}$

2. $6 + 6 = \underline{\quad}$ $7 + 6 = \underline{\quad}$ $6 + 7 = \underline{\quad}$

3. $8 + 8 = \underline{\quad}$ $9 + 8 = \underline{\quad}$ $8 + 9 = \underline{\quad}$

4. $\begin{array}{r} 4 \\ +5 \\ \hline \end{array}$
5. $\begin{array}{r} 3 \\ +3 \\ \hline \end{array}$
6. $\begin{array}{r} 4 \\ +3 \\ \hline \end{array}$
7. $\begin{array}{r} 5 \\ +5 \\ \hline \end{array}$
8. $\begin{array}{r} 6 \\ +5 \\ \hline \end{array}$
9. $\begin{array}{r} 6 \\ +6 \\ \hline \end{array}$

10. $\begin{array}{r} 4 \\ +4 \\ \hline \end{array}$
11. $\begin{array}{r} 5 \\ +4 \\ \hline \end{array}$
12. $\begin{array}{r} 3 \\ +4 \\ \hline \end{array}$
13. $\begin{array}{r} 7 \\ +6 \\ \hline \end{array}$
14. $\begin{array}{r} 8 \\ +7 \\ \hline \end{array}$
15. $\begin{array}{r} 9 \\ +10 \\ \hline \end{array}$

16. $\begin{array}{r} 7 \\ +7 \\ \hline \end{array}$
17. $\begin{array}{r} 9 \\ +9 \\ \hline \end{array}$
18. $\begin{array}{r} 7 \\ +8 \\ \hline \end{array}$
19. $\begin{array}{r} 6 \\ +7 \\ \hline \end{array}$
20. $\begin{array}{r} 9 \\ +8 \\ \hline \end{array}$
21. $\begin{array}{r} 10 \\ +9 \\ \hline \end{array}$

Problem Solving ▶ Reasoning

22. Kate wants to put the coins into equal groups. Circle groups of coins to show one way she can do this.

At Home Have your child tell you the sum for 6 + 5 and 5 + 6.
Ask what double fact helps to find the sums.

Name _____

Add With Ten

Objective
Add numbers 1 through 10 to the number 10.

Use ten frames to add a number to 10.
Find 10 + 4.

Show 10.

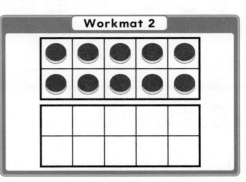

Show 4 more.

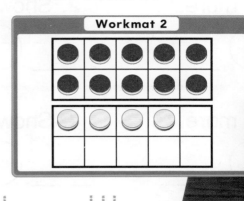

$\underline{}10\underline{} + \underline{}4\underline{} = \underline{}14\underline{}$

Guided Practice

Use Workmat 2 and .
Show the numbers.
Write the number sentence.

Think
Count on 2 more from 10.

1. Show 10. Show 2 more.

   ____ ◯ ____ ◯ ____

2. Show 10. Show 6 more.

   ____ ◯ ____ ◯ ____

3. Show 10. Show 8 more.

   ____ ◯ ____ ◯ ____

4. Show 10. Show 1 more.

   ____ ◯ ____ ◯ ____

5. Show 10. Show 5 more.

   ____ ◯ ____ ◯ ____

TEST TIPS **Explain Your Thinking** How is adding 10 + 5 like showing 15 with 1 ten and 5 ones?

Remember to fill one
ten frame first.

Use Workmat 2 and .
Show the numbers.
Write the number sentence.

1. Show 10. Show 7 more.

10 (+) 7 (show more) 17

2. Show 10. Show 3 more.

___ ◯ ___ ◯ ___

3. Show 10. Show 9 more.

___ ◯ ___ ◯ ___

4. Show 10. Show 10 more.

___ ◯ ___ ◯ ___

Find the sum.

5.
$$\begin{array}{r} 10 \\ + 3 \\ \hline \end{array}$$

6.
$$\begin{array}{r} 3 \\ +10 \\ \hline \end{array}$$

7.
$$\begin{array}{r} 10 \\ + 4 \\ \hline \end{array}$$

8.
$$\begin{array}{r} 9 \\ +10 \\ \hline \end{array}$$

9.
$$\begin{array}{r} 10 \\ + 7 \\ \hline \end{array}$$

10.
$$\begin{array}{r} 8 \\ +2 \\ \hline \end{array}$$

11.
$$\begin{array}{r} 2 \\ +10 \\ \hline \end{array}$$

12.
$$\begin{array}{r} 10 \\ + 5 \\ \hline \end{array}$$

13.
$$\begin{array}{r} 10 \\ + 8 \\ \hline \end{array}$$

14.
$$\begin{array}{r} 10 \\ + 9 \\ \hline \end{array}$$

15.
$$\begin{array}{r} 1 \\ +9 \\ \hline \end{array}$$

16.
$$\begin{array}{r} 10 \\ + 6 \\ \hline \end{array}$$

17.
$$\begin{array}{r} 10 \\ +10 \\ \hline \end{array}$$

18.
$$\begin{array}{r} 10 \\ + 2 \\ \hline \end{array}$$

19.
$$\begin{array}{r} 4 \\ +10 \\ \hline \end{array}$$

Algebra Readiness ▶ Number Sentences

Write a related subtraction fact for the addition fact.

20. $5 + 6 = 11$

____ − ____ = ____

21. $7 + 5 = 12$

____ − ____ = ____

At Home Say a number between 1 and 10. Ask your child to
add it to 10 to find the sum. Repeat with other numbers.

Name_____

Make a Ten to Add

 **MathTracks 2/22**
Listen and Understand

Objective
Make a 10 as a strategy to learn addition facts.

Make a **10** to help you add with **7**, **8**, or **9**.

Find **8 + 4**.

Show **8** and **4** more.   Move **2** counters to make **10**.

Think about 8 + 2 = 10.

8 + 4 has the same sum as 10 + 2.

8 + 4   10 + 2   8 + 4 = __12__

Guided Practice

Use Workmat 2 and .

Make a ten.

Find the sum.

> **Think**
> Move 1 counter to make a 10. 9 + 6 has the same sum as 10 + 5.

1. Show **9** and **6** more.

   9 + 6 = _____

2. Show **8** and **5** more.

   8 + 5 = _____

3. Show **9** and **4** more.

   9 + 4 = _____

4. Show **9** and **5** more.

   9 + 5 = _____

5. Show **8** and **3** more.

   8 + 3 = _____

TEST TIPS **Explain Your Thinking** How does making a **10** help you add **9 + 5**?

Remember to make a 10 first.

Use Workmat 2 and ⬭.
Make a ten. Find the sum.

1. Show **8** and **6** more.

    8 + 6 = __14__

2. Show **7** and **5** more.

    7 + 5 = _____

3. Show **9** and **7** more.

    9 + 7 = _____

4. Show **8** and **7** more.

    8 + 7 = _____

Add.

5. 7
    +4

6. 7
    +5

7. 7
    +6

8. 7
    +7

9. 7
    +8

10. 7
    +9

11. 8
    +4

12. 8
    +5

13. 8
    +6

14. 8
    +7

15. 8
    +8

16. 8
    +9

17. 9
    +4

18. 9
    +5

19. 9
    +6

20. 9
    +7

21. 9
    +8

22. 9
    +9

Problem Solving ▶ Reasoning

23. Raja scores **9** points.
    Then he scores **8** more.
    How many points does
    he have now?

    Draw or write to explain.

    _____ points

At Home Ask your child how he or she could make a 10 to help add 7 + 6.

Go on ➡

Totally Twelve

2 Players

What You Need: pencil and paper clips

How to Play

1. Take turns.

2. Spin the spinner.

3. Complete the number sentence to show the sum is 12.

4. Cover the two addends on your number strip with paper clips.

5. Continue taking turns until one player covers the whole number strip.

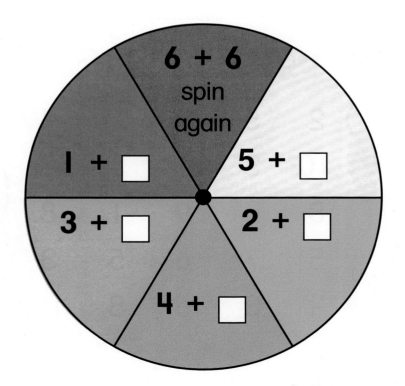

Player 1	Player 2
1	1
2	2
3	3
4	4
5	5
6+6	6+6
7	7
8	8
9	9
10	10
11	11

Quick Check

Find the sum.

1. 6 + 6 = _____   6 + 7 = _____   7 + 6 = _____

2. 8 + 8 = _____   8 + 9 = _____   9 + 8 = _____

3.   1 0
   +   5
   _____

4.   1 0
   +   4
   _____

5.   4
   +1 0
   _____

6.   1 0
   +   9
   _____

Use Workmat 2 and .

Make a ten. Find the sum.

7. Show 9 and 5 more.

   9 + 5 = _____

8. Show 7 and 6 more.

   7 + 6 = _____

Math Challenge

Number Neighbors

Look for two numbers next to each other that have a sum of 13.

Find as many as you can. Circle the numbers you find.

2	5	8	7	4
10	3	1	6	9
8	4	9	1	8
5	7	6	5	3
4	3	6	8	10

Addition Practice

Objective
Use different strategies to practice addition.

Use counters to add $6 + 5$.

Use parts and wholes.

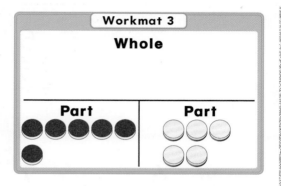

Use a double fact.

$5 + 5 = \underline{10}$

Draw 1 more.

Use a ten frame.

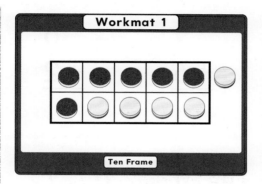

$\underline{6} + \underline{5} = \underline{11}$

Guided Practice

Choose a way to add.
Find the sum.

Think
Make a ten.
Then add $10 + 2$.

1. $9 + 3 = \underline{\hspace{1cm}}$

2. $8 + 6 = \underline{\hspace{1cm}}$

3. $8 + 8 = \underline{\hspace{1cm}}$ 4. $1 + 9 = \underline{\hspace{1cm}}$ 5. $9 + 8 = \underline{\hspace{1cm}}$

6. $\begin{array}{r} 3 \\ +8 \\ \hline \end{array}$ 7. $\begin{array}{r} 6 \\ +6 \\ \hline \end{array}$ 8. $\begin{array}{r} 5 \\ +5 \\ \hline \end{array}$ 9. $\begin{array}{r} 4 \\ +8 \\ \hline \end{array}$ 10. $\begin{array}{r} 4 \\ +9 \\ \hline \end{array}$ 11. $\begin{array}{r} 5 \\ +6 \\ \hline \end{array}$

TEST TIPS **Explain Your Thinking** How did you add $5 + 6$?

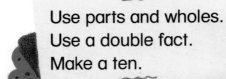
Use parts and wholes.
Use a double fact.
Make a ten.

Choose a way to add.
Find the sum.

1. $8 + 9 = \underline{17}$ 2. $6 + 3 = \underline{}$ 3. $4 + 7 = \underline{}$

4. $\begin{array}{r} 7 \\ +6 \\ \hline \end{array}$ 5. $\begin{array}{r} 9 \\ +2 \\ \hline \end{array}$ 6. $\begin{array}{r} 7 \\ +8 \\ \hline \end{array}$ 7. $\begin{array}{r} 6 \\ +5 \\ \hline \end{array}$ 8. $\begin{array}{r} 7 \\ +3 \\ \hline \end{array}$ 9. $\begin{array}{r} 5 \\ +5 \\ \hline \end{array}$

10. $\begin{array}{r} 4 \\ +6 \\ \hline \end{array}$ 11. $\begin{array}{r} 9 \\ +1 \\ \hline \end{array}$ 12. $\begin{array}{r} 5 \\ +7 \\ \hline \end{array}$ 13. $\begin{array}{r} 2 \\ +9 \\ \hline \end{array}$ 14. $\begin{array}{r} 6 \\ +7 \\ \hline \end{array}$ 15. $\begin{array}{r} 7 \\ +7 \\ \hline \end{array}$

16. $\begin{array}{r} 4 \\ +8 \\ \hline \end{array}$ 17. $\begin{array}{r} 8 \\ +7 \\ \hline \end{array}$ 18. $\begin{array}{r} 9 \\ +9 \\ \hline \end{array}$ 19. $\begin{array}{r} 9 \\ +5 \\ \hline \end{array}$ 20. $\begin{array}{r} 10 \\ +9 \\ \hline \end{array}$ 21. $\begin{array}{r} 9 \\ +6 \\ \hline \end{array}$

Problem Solving **Number Sense**

> **Remember**
> \> is greater than
> < is less than
> = is equal to

Compare.
Circle >, <, or =.

22. $\boxed{18}$ > < = $\boxed{81}$

23. $\boxed{65}$ > < = $\boxed{65}$

24. $\boxed{96}$ > < = $\boxed{69}$

At Home Review the addition exercises above.
Have your child use pennies to help with sums that are difficult.

Name_____

Names for Numbers

 MathTracks 2/23
Listen and Understand

There are different ways to make the same sum.
Use counters to find different names for 14.

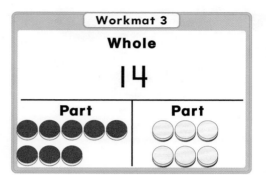

Workmat 3
Whole
14

Part	Part

Whole 14	Whole 14
Part	Part	Part	Part
8	6	6	8

Whole 14	Whole 14	Whole 14
Part	Part	Part	Part	Part	Part
7	7	5	9	9	5

Guided Practice

Use Workmat 3 and 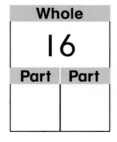.
Find different names for the number.

1.

Whole 16	Whole 16	Whole 16
Part	Part	Part	Part	Part	Part

Think
What is the double fact for 16?

2.

Whole 12	Whole 12	Whole 12	Whole 12	Whole 12
Part	Part	Part	Part	Part	Part	Part	Part	Part	Part

TEST TIPS **Explain Your Thinking** Tell why 9 + 3 is not a name for 14.

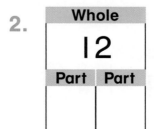

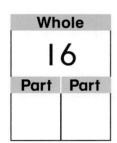

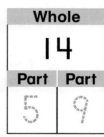

Objective
Use parts and wholes to find different names for the same number.

Hands-On

Chapter 19 Lesson 5

five hundred sixty-seven **567**

Remember to check that the parts equal the whole.

Use Workmat 3 and ⬭.
Find different names for the number.

1.

Whole	
17	
Part	**Part**
9	8

Whole	
17	
Part	**Part**
8	9

2.

Whole	
15	
Part	**Part**

Whole	
15	
Part	**Part**

Whole	
15	
Part	**Part**

Whole	
15	
Part	**Part**

3.

Whole	
13	
Part	**Part**

Whole	
13	
Part	**Part**

Whole	
13	
Part	**Part**

Whole	
13	
Part	**Part**

Whole	
13	
Part	**Part**

Whole	
13	
Part	**Part**

Algebra Readiness ▶ Missing Addends

Find the missing part.

4.

Whole	
17	
Part	**Part**
9	

5.

Whole	
18	
Part	**Part**
	9

6.

Whole	
14	
Part	**Part**
5	

🏠 **At Home** Help your child find different names for the numbers 10 and 11.

Add Three Numbers

 **MathTracks 2/24**
Listen and Understand

Objective
Find the sum of three numbers.

When you add three numbers look for a fact you know.

Use doubles.	Make a 10.	Add in any order.

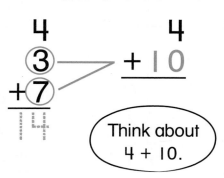

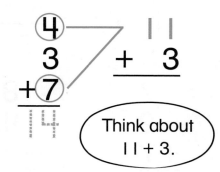

Think about 7 + 7.

Think about 4 + 10.

Think about 11 + 3.

Guided Practice

Look for a fact you know.
Find the sum.

1. 8
    2
  +4   + ☐

Think
I know 8 + 2.
I write that sum
and add 4.

2. 9
    5
  +1   + ☐

3. 7
    8
  +2   + ☐

4. 2
    6
  +6   + ☐

5. 6
    7
  +4   + ☐

6. $2 + 8 + 9 = $ _____

7. $8 + 0 + 4 = $ _____

TEST TIPS **Explain Your Thinking** How did you find the sum in Exercise 7?

Look for a fact you know. Then add the third number.

Find the sum.

1. 6
    6
    +4
    ──
    16

2. 3
    3
    +6
    ──

3. 6
    3
    +4
    ──

4. 10
     1
    + 3
    ──

5. 3
    7
    +7
    ──

6. 6
    8
    +1
    ──

7. 7
    2
    +7
    ──

8. 8
    4
    +4
    ──

9. 9
    6
    +1
    ──

10. 8
    7
    +3
    ──

11. 1
    9
    +7
    ──

12. 9
    9
    +1
    ──

13. 2 + 8 + 2 = _____

14. 3 + 5 + 8 = _____

15. 6 + 5 + 4 = _____

16. 4 + 9 + 6 = _____

17. 5 + 5 + 5 = _____

18. 7 + 1 + 7 = _____

Problem Solving ▶ Data Sense

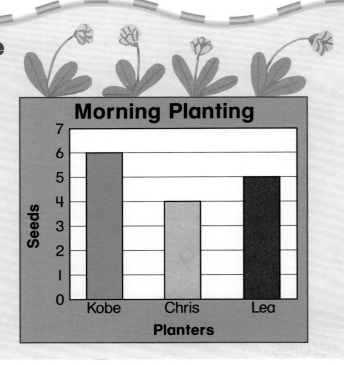

19. Kobe plants 5 seeds in the afternoon. How many total seeds does he plant?

    _____ seeds

20. **Talk About It** Create a story problem about the seeds planted by Chris and Lea.

Morning Planting

Seeds / Planters: Kobe 6, Chris 4, Lea 5

At Home Give your child 3 numbers less than 10. Ask him or her to tell you the sum.

Name_____

Write a Number Sentence

Sue and Lee plant a garden.
They each plant **9** watermelon
seeds. How many watermelon
seeds do they plant altogether?

Objective
Write a number
sentence to solve
a problem.

What do you know?

- Sue plants **9** watermelon seeds.
- Lee plants **9** watermelon seeds.

PLAN

How can you find how many in all?

You know the
parts. You can add to
find the whole.

Whole	
Number of seeds in all	
Part	**Part**
9	9

add

SOLVE

Write a number sentence.

<u>9</u> (<u>+</u>) <u>9</u> (<u>=</u>) <u>18</u> watermelon seeds

LOOK BACK

Does your addition sentence show the two parts?
Does the sum show how many there are altogether?

Guided Practice

Write a number sentence to solve.

1. The Greens bring 8 ears of corn to the picnic. The Riveras bring 7. How many ears of corn do they bring in all?

   Think
   I add to find how many ears of corn in all.

   ____ ◯ ____ ◯ ____

   _____ ears of corn

2. The Clarks sell 5 melons. The Hales sell 4 melons. How many melons do they sell altogether?

   Think
   I add to find how many melons altogether.

   ____ ◯ ____ ◯ ____

   _____ melons

Practice

3. Luke picks 6 peppers. Donna picks 8 peppers. How many peppers do they pick in all?

   ____ ◯ ____ ◯ ____

   _____ peppers

4. **Multistep** Kasey plants 1 row of pumpkin seeds. Then she plants 1 row of squash seeds. Each row has 10 seeds. How many seeds does she plant?

   ____ ◯ ____ ◯ ____

   _____ seeds

Go on

Name_____

Vocabulary *e* Glossary

Complete the sentence.

double
related facts

1. 6 + 7 and 7 + 6 are _____.

2. 8 + 8 is a _____ fact.

Concepts and Skills

Find the sum.

3. 6 + 6 = _____   6 + 7 = _____   7 + 6 = _____

4. 8 + 8 = _____   8 + 9 = _____   9 + 8 = _____

Use Workmat 2 and .
Show the numbers.
Write the number sentence.

5. Show 10. Show 5 more.

___ ◯ ___ ◯ ___

6. Show 10. Show 2 more.

___ ◯ ___ ◯ ___

Add.

7. 9
   +7

8. 9
   +5

9. 8
   +4

10. 8
   +5

11. 7
   +4

12. 10
   + 5

13. 6
   +7

14. 2
   +9

15. 9
   +9

16. 7
   +7

Use Workmat 3 and .
Find different names for the number.

17.
Whole	
14	
Part	Part

18.
Whole	
14	
Part	Part

19.
Whole	
14	
Part	Part

20.
Whole	
14	
Part	Part

Find the sum.

21.
$$\begin{array}{r} 7 \\ 7 \\ +3 \\ \hline \end{array}$$

22.
$$\begin{array}{r} 1 \\ 8 \\ +2 \\ \hline \end{array}$$

23.
$$\begin{array}{r} 4 \\ 5 \\ +4 \\ \hline \end{array}$$

24.
$$\begin{array}{r} 7 \\ 3 \\ +5 \\ \hline \end{array}$$

25.
$$\begin{array}{r} 9 \\ 9 \\ +1 \\ \hline \end{array}$$

26. $5 + 5 + 6 = $ _____

27. $9 + 4 + 1 = $ _____

28. $7 + 3 + 3 = $ _____

29. $8 + 8 + 2 = $ _____

Problem Solving

Write a number sentence to solve.

30. Tony's team has 10 bats. They buy 5 more. How many bats do they have now?

_____ ◯ _____ ◯ _____

_____ bats

Subtraction Facts Through 20

CHAPTER 20

INVESTIGATION

Mr. Rabbit needs to use 4 carrots in his soup. How many will he have left?

Subtraction Soup

Use .
Find the missing part.
Complete the number sentence.

Whole

Part | **Part**

12 − 8 = _____   10 − 7 = _____

11 − _____ = 5   12 − _____ = 9

Name_____

Use Doubles to Subtract

Addition and subtraction are related.
Use addition to help you subtract.

Use a double fact to help you subtract.

Find 14 − 7.

You know 7 + 7 = 14.

So, 14 − 7 = __7__.

Guided Practice

Add.
Then subtract.

Think
Use 9 + 9 to find 18 − 9.

1.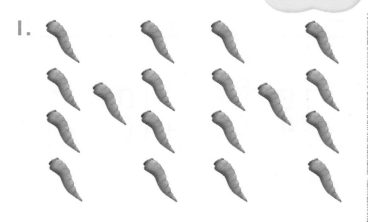

9 + 9 = _____

18 − 9 = _____

2.

10 + 10 = _____

20 − 10 = _____

3. 8   16   4. 6   12   5. 5   10
   +8   − 8   +6   − 6   +5   − 5
   ___   ____   ___   ____   ___   ____

TEST TIPS **Explain Your Thinking** Why are 5 + 5 = 10 and
10 − 5 = 5 related facts?

Practice

Use the double fact to help you subtract.

Add. Then subtract.

1. $1 + 1 = \underline{2}$
   $2 - 1 = \underline{1}$

2. $2 + 2 = \underline{}$
   $4 - 2 = \underline{}$

3. $3 + 3 = \underline{}$
   $6 - 3 = \underline{}$

4. $4 + 4 = \underline{}$
   $8 - 4 = \underline{}$

5. $5 + 5 = \underline{}$
   $10 - 5 = \underline{}$

6. $6 + 6 = \underline{}$
   $12 - 6 = \underline{}$

7. $7 + 7 = \underline{}$
   $14 - 7 = \underline{}$

8. $8 + 8 = \underline{}$
   $16 - 8 = \underline{}$

9. $9 + 9 = \underline{}$
   $18 - 9 = \underline{}$

10. $\begin{array}{r} 5 \\ +5 \\ \hline \end{array}$ $\begin{array}{r} 10 \\ -5 \\ \hline \end{array}$

11. $\begin{array}{r} 6 \\ +6 \\ \hline \end{array}$ $\begin{array}{r} 12 \\ -6 \\ \hline \end{array}$

12. $\begin{array}{r} 7 \\ +7 \\ \hline \end{array}$ $\begin{array}{r} 14 \\ -7 \\ \hline \end{array}$

13. $\begin{array}{r} 8 \\ +8 \\ \hline \end{array}$ $\begin{array}{r} 16 \\ -8 \\ \hline \end{array}$

14. $\begin{array}{r} 9 \\ +9 \\ \hline \end{array}$ $\begin{array}{r} 18 \\ -9 \\ \hline \end{array}$

15. $\begin{array}{r} 10 \\ +10 \\ \hline \end{array}$ $\begin{array}{r} 20 \\ -10 \\ \hline \end{array}$

Problem Solving ▶ Reasoning

16. Bonnie has these coins. What other coins does she need to make 41¢?

17. **Talk About It** How did you find the answer?

At Home Ask your child to name a double fact and give the related subtraction fact.

Subtract From 13 and 14

A related fact can help you find the **difference.**

Objective
Subtract from 13 and 14, using related addition facts.
Vocabulary
difference

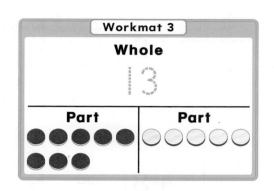

$$\begin{array}{r} 8 \\ +5 \\ \hline 13 \end{array}$$

$$\begin{array}{r} 13 \\ -\ 8 \\ \hline 5 \end{array}$$

$$\begin{array}{r} 13 \\ -\ 5 \\ \hline 8 \end{array}$$

These facts are related because they have the same parts and wholes.

Guided Practice

Add.

Then find the differences.

Think
I can use 8 + 6 to find 14 − 6 and 14 − 8.

1.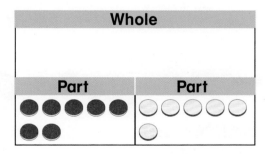

$$\begin{array}{r} 8 \\ +6 \\ \hline \end{array}$$

$$\begin{array}{r} 14 \\ -\ 6 \\ \hline \end{array}$$

$$\begin{array}{r} 14 \\ -\ 8 \\ \hline \end{array}$$

2.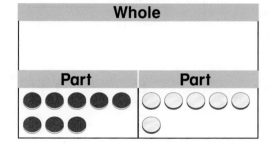

$$\begin{array}{r} 7 \\ +6 \\ \hline \end{array}$$

$$\begin{array}{r} 13 \\ -\ 7 \\ \hline \end{array}$$

$$\begin{array}{r} 13 \\ -\ 6 \\ \hline \end{array}$$

3. $\begin{array}{r} 9 \\ +5 \\ \hline \end{array}$ $\begin{array}{r} 14 \\ -\ 9 \\ \hline \end{array}$ $\begin{array}{r} 14 \\ -\ 5 \\ \hline \end{array}$

4. $\begin{array}{r} 9 \\ +4 \\ \hline \end{array}$ $\begin{array}{r} 13 \\ -\ 9 \\ \hline \end{array}$ $\begin{array}{r} 13 \\ -\ 4 \\ \hline \end{array}$

TEST TIPS **Explain Your Thinking** What addition fact can help you find $12 - 6$? Why?

Remember to use the addition fact to help you subtract.

Add.
Then find the differences.

1.
```
   1 0
 +   3
 ─────
   1 3
```
```
   1 3
 − 1 0
 ─────
     3
```
```
   1 3
 −   3
 ─────
   1 0
```

2.
```
   4
 +8
 ───
```
```
   1 2
 −   4
 ─────
```
```
   1 2
 −   8
 ─────
```

3.
```
   7
 +6
 ───
```
```
   1 3
 −   7
 ─────
```
```
   1 3
 −   6
 ─────
```

4.
```
   5
 +8
 ───
```
```
   1 3
 −   5
 ─────
```
```
   1 3
 −   8
 ─────
```

5.
```
   4
 +9
 ───
```
```
   1 3
 −   4
 ─────
```
```
   1 3
 −   9
 ─────
```

6.
```
   9
 +3
 ───
```
```
   1 2
 −   9
 ─────
```
```
   1 2
 −   3
 ─────
```

7.
```
   6
 +8
 ───
```
```
   1 4
 −   6
 ─────
```
```
   1 4
 −   8
 ─────
```

8.
```
   5
 +9
 ───
```
```
   1 4
 −   5
 ─────
```
```
   1 4
 −   9
 ─────
```

Algebra Readiness ▶ Number Sentences

Write an addition sentence to match the picture.
Then write the related subtraction sentences.

9. _____ + _____ = _____

10. _____ − _____ = _____

11. _____ − _____ = _____

At Home Ask your child to subtract 5 and 6 from 13 and 14.

Subtract From 15 and 16

Objective
Subtract from 15 and 16 by using related addition facts.

Use an addition fact to help you subtract.

```
   8
 + 7
 ─────
  15
```

Workmat 3

Whole
15

Part	Part

```
  15
-  8
─────
   7
```

```
  15
-  7
─────
   8
```

Guided Practice

Add.

Then find the differences.

1.
```
   9
 + 7
```

Whole

Part	Part

Think
Use 9 + 7 = 16.

```
  16
-  9
```

```
  16
-  7
```

2.
```
   9
 + 6
```

Whole

Part	Part

```
  15
-  9
```

```
  15
-  6
```

3.
```
  10
+  5
```
```
  15
-10
```
```
  15
-  5
```

4.
```
  10
+  6
```
```
  16
-10
```
```
  16
-  6
```

TEST TIPS **Explain Your Thinking** If you know 10 + 6 = 16, what two related subtraction facts do you know?

Remember to use the addition fact to help you subtract.

Add.
Then find the differences.

1.
```
  7      16      16
+ 9    −  7    −  9
 16       9       7
```

2.
```
  5      14      14
+ 9    −  9    −  5
```

3.
```
 10      12      12
+ 2    − 10    −  2
```

4.
```
  5      13      13
+ 8    −  5    −  8
```

5.
```
  5      15      15
+10    −  5    − 10
```

6.
```
  6      15      15
+ 9    −  6    −  9
```

7.
```
  7      15      15
+ 8    −  7    −  8
```

8.
```
  6      16      16
+10    −  6    − 10
```

Reading Math ▶ Vocabulary

Write a number word to complete the sentence.

9. Fifteen minus nine equals _____.

10. Sixteen minus seven equals _____.

At Home Ask your child to name the addition facts that can help solve 16 − 9 and 15 − 8.

Go on ➡

Writing Math:
Create and Solve

Draw 15 tomatoes in a garden.

Color some [crayon] .

Color the rest [crayon] .

My Garden

Write two addition and two subtraction sentences that you can solve with your picture.

1. ____ ◯ ____ ◯ ____

2. ____ ◯ ____ ◯ ____

3. ____ ◯ ____ ◯ ____

4. ____ ◯ ____ ◯ ____

Quick Check

Add. Then subtract.

1. $8 + 8 =$ _____

   $16 - 8 =$ _____

2. $9 + 9 =$ _____

   $18 - 9 =$ _____

3.
```
   6        12
  +6       - 6
```

4.
```
   7        14
  +7       - 7
```

5.
```
   5
  +8
```

Whole	
Part	**Part**
●●●●●	○○○○○ ○○○

```
  13       13
 - 5      - 8
```

6.
```
   6      15       15
  +9     - 6      - 9
```

7.
```
   9      16       16
  +7     - 9      - 7
```

Math Challenge

Triangle Puzzle

In this triangle puzzle you get the same sum when you add the numbers along each side.

Fill in the missing numbers so the sum on each side is 9.

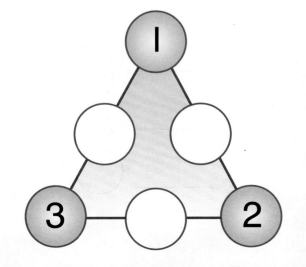

Name_____

Subtract From 17 Through 20

Use an addition fact to help you subtract.

Objective
Subtract from 17 through 20 by relating addition to subtraction.

$$\begin{array}{r} 9 \\ +8 \\ \hline 17 \end{array}$$

Workmat 3

Whole

17

Part	Part
●●●●●	○○○○○
●●●●	○○○

$$\begin{array}{r} 17 \\ -9 \\ \hline 8 \end{array}$$

$$\begin{array}{r} 17 \\ -8 \\ \hline 9 \end{array}$$

Guided Practice

Add.
Then subtract.

1.
$$\begin{array}{r} 9 \\ +9 \\ \hline \end{array}$$

Whole

Part	Part
●●●●●	○○○○○
●●●●	○○○

Think
Use 9 + 9 to find the related fact.

$$\begin{array}{r} 18 \\ -9 \\ \hline \end{array}$$

2.
$$\begin{array}{r} 10 \\ +10 \\ \hline \end{array}$$

Whole

Part	Part
●●●●●	○○○○○
●●●●●	○○○○○

$$\begin{array}{r} 20 \\ -10 \\ \hline \end{array}$$

3.
$$\begin{array}{r} 17 \\ -9 \\ \hline \end{array}$$

4.
$$\begin{array}{r} 18 \\ -8 \\ \hline \end{array}$$

5.
$$\begin{array}{r} 17 \\ -10 \\ \hline \end{array}$$

6.
$$\begin{array}{r} 19 \\ -9 \\ \hline \end{array}$$

7.
$$\begin{array}{r} 18 \\ -10 \\ \hline \end{array}$$

8.
$$\begin{array}{r} 19 \\ -10 \\ \hline \end{array}$$

TEST TIPS **Explain Your Thinking** Why is it easy to add and subtract with 10?

Use addition to help you subtract.

Subtract.

1. 18 − 9
9

2. 17 − 9

3. 18 − 8

4. 16 − 7

5. 19 − 9

6. 15 − 6

7. 16 − 6

8. 16 − 8

9. 17 − 8

10. 17 − 7

11. 16 − 9

12. 15 − 9

13. 14 − 9

14. 13 − 9

15. 12 − 9

16. 20 − 10

17. 19 − 10

18. 18 − 10

19. 17 − 10

20. 16 − 10

21. **Talk About It** Find the pattern in the last row.

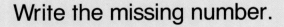

Algebra Readiness ▶ Missing Numbers

Write the missing number.

22. 19 − ⬚ = 9

23. 20 − ⬚ = 10

24. 17 − ⬚ = 8

25. 18 − ⬚ = 9

At Home Review subtraction with your child. Read exercises from this page and have your child find the differences.

Relate Addition and Subtraction

MathTracks 2/25
Listen and Understand

Objective
Find missing addends by relating addition and subtraction.

Use related addition facts to help you subtract.

Find 13 − 9.

9 plus what number equals 13?

9 + __4__ = 13

so

13 − 9 = __4__

Guided Practice

Write the missing numbers.

1. 15 − 7 = _____

   7 + _____ = 15

Think
What number can I add to 7 to get 15?

2. 13 − 8 = _____

   8 + _____ = 13

3. 15 − 9 = _____

   9 + _____ = 15

4. 16 − 8 = _____

   8 + _____ = 16

5. 16 − 9 = _____

   9 + _____ = 16

TEST TIPS **Explain Your Thinking** What number can you add to 7 to get 13? Name the related subtraction facts.

Practice

Remember to use the related addition and subtraction facts.

Write the missing numbers.

1. 18 − 9 = _9_

   9 + _9_ = 18

2. 12 − 9 = ___

   9 + ___ = 12

3. 16 − 7 = ___

   7 + ___ = 16

4. 15 − 8 = ___

   8 + ___ = 15

5. 14 − 9 = ___

   9 + ___ = 14

6. 13 − 7 = ___

   7 + ___ = 13

7. 13 − 4 = ___

   4 + ___ = 13

8. 12 − 6 = ___

   6 + ___ = 12

9. 12 − 4 = ___

   4 + ___ = 12

10. 17 − 8 = ___

    8 + ___ = 17

11. 15 − 6 = ___

    6 + ___ = 15

12. 20 − 10 = ___

    10 + ___ = 20

Algebra Readiness ▶ Number Sentences

Use the code.
Complete the number sentence.

Code
 = 8    = 9

13.  + = _____

14.  + = _____

15. **Write About It** Make up a code. Write your own problem.

_____

_____

At Home Ask your child to name addition facts that can help solve 15 − 9 and 17 − 8.

Fact Families

MathTracks 2/26
Listen and Understand

Use related facts to make a fact family.

These 4 facts make a fact family.

15
8 | 7

| 8 + 7 = 15 | 7 + 8 = 15 | 15 − 8 = 7 | 15 − 7 = 8 |

Guided Practice

Complete the fact family.

Think
All the facts in this family use the numbers 13, 7, and 6.

1.
13
7 | 6

7 + 6 = ☐   ☐ + ☐ = ☐   13 − 7 = ☐   ☐ − ☐ = ☐

2.
14
9 | 5

9 + 5 = ☐   ☐ + ☐ = ☐   14 − 9 = ☐   ☐ − ☐ = ☐

TEST TIPS **Explain Your Thinking** What is the fact family for 8, 9, and 17?

Remember that each fact family has the same numbers.

Complete the fact family.

1.

$\begin{array}{r} 9 \\ + 8 \\ \hline 17 \end{array}$ $\begin{array}{r} 8 \\ + 9 \\ \hline 17 \end{array}$ $\begin{array}{r} 17 \\ - 9 \\ \hline 8 \end{array}$ $\begin{array}{r} 17 \\ - 8 \\ \hline 9 \end{array}$

2.

$\begin{array}{r} 8 \\ + 5 \\ \hline \end{array}$ $\begin{array}{r} \\ + \\ \hline \end{array}$ $\begin{array}{r} 13 \\ - 8 \\ \hline \end{array}$ $\begin{array}{r} \\ - \\ \hline \end{array}$

3.

$\begin{array}{r} 8 \\ + 6 \\ \hline \end{array}$ $\begin{array}{r} \\ + \\ \hline \end{array}$ $\begin{array}{r} 14 \\ - 8 \\ \hline \end{array}$ $\begin{array}{r} \\ - \\ \hline \end{array}$

Problem Solving ▶ Visual Thinking

4. Find the numbers that are outside the circle but inside the square. Use them to write a fact family.

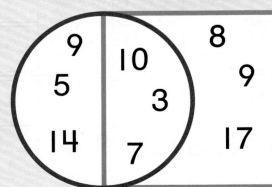

____ + ____ = ____

____ + ____ = ____

____ − ____ = ____

____ − ____ = ____

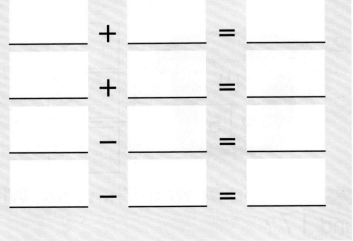

At Home Ask your child to write a fact family using the numbers 13, 9, and 4.

Too Much Information

 MathTracks 2/27
Listen and Understand

Objective
Solve problems with too much information.

Some problems have more information than you need.

17 eels are in the lagoon.
9 catfish are in the lagoon.
8 eels are black.

How many more eels than catfish are there?

Decide what information you need.

THINK

Do I need to know that there are 17 eels?

Do I need to know that there are 9 catfish?

Do I need to know that 8 of the eels are black?

DECIDE

Yes. I need to compare the number of eels to the number of catfish.

Yes. I need to know the number of catfish.

No. I need to know the number of eels, not the color.

17 eels are in the lagoon.
9 catfish are in the lagoon.
~~8 eels are black.~~

Cross out the extra information.

How many more eels than catfish are there?

Subtract to compare the numbers.

___17___ – ___9___ = ___8___   8 more eels

Cross out information you do not need.

Solve.

1. 16 trout are near the shore.
   ~~There are 10 kinds of fish in the lake.~~
   8 trout swim away.
   How many trout
   are near the shore now?

   Think
   What information
   do I need to solve
   the problem?

   Draw or write to explain.

   ___8___ trout

2. 18 codfish swim by the dock.
   9 codfish swim away.
   How many codfish
   are by the dock now?

   Think
   Do I need to know
   how many codfish
   swim away?

   _____ codfish

Practice

3. There are 15 crabs on the
   beach. Crabs have 10 legs.
   6 crabs crawl into the water.
   How many crabs are left on
   the beach?

   _____ crabs

4. Sue finds 13 clams. Sam
   finds 9 clams. How many
   more clams does Sue find
   than Sam?

   _____ more clams

At Home Create a subtraction story problem. Include extra
information. Ask your child to solve the problem.

Quick Check

Add.
Then subtract.

1.　$\begin{array}{r} 8 \\ +9 \\ \hline \end{array}$　$\begin{array}{r} 17 \\ -8 \\ \hline \end{array}$　$\begin{array}{r} 17 \\ -9 \\ \hline \end{array}$　　2.　$\begin{array}{r} 10 \\ +10 \\ \hline \end{array}$　$\begin{array}{r} 20 \\ -10 \\ \hline \end{array}$

Write the missing numbers.

3.　$18 - 9 = $ _____

　　$9 + $ _____ $= 18$

4.　$16 - 9 = $ _____

　　$9 + $ _____ $= 16$

Complete the fact family.

5.

$+$ $\begin{array}{c}\boxed{7} \\ \boxed{8} \\ \hline \boxed{}\end{array}$　$+$ $\begin{array}{c}\boxed{} \\ \boxed{} \\ \hline \boxed{}\end{array}$　$-$ $\begin{array}{c}\boxed{15} \\ \boxed{7} \\ \hline \boxed{}\end{array}$　$-$ $\begin{array}{c}\boxed{} \\ \boxed{} \\ \hline \boxed{}\end{array}$

Cross out information you do not need.
Solve.

6. Marco catches 14 crabs.
The crab cage can hold
about 20 crabs. He lets 6
crabs go. How many crabs
does Marco have now?

Draw or write to explain.

_____ crabs

Write the number in different ways.

1.

_____ tens _____ ones

_____ + _____ = _____

2.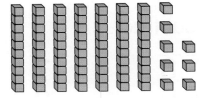

_____ tens _____ ones

_____ + _____ = _____

3.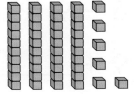

_____ tens _____ ones

_____ + _____ = _____

4.

_____ tens _____ ones

_____ + _____ = _____

Science Connection

Animal Groups

Groups of animals have special names.
Cattle live in a herd. Some fish swim
in a school. Whales live in a pod.

The Chuns see two pods of whales.
One pod has 9 whales.
The other pod has 7 whales.

How many more whales are in the larger pod?   _____ whales

Name_____

Vocabulary *e* ▸ Glossary

Complete the sentence.

difference	fact family

1. A _____ has related addition and subtraction facts.

2. Subtract to find the _____.

Concepts and Skills

Add.

Then subtract.

3. 5 + 5 = ____

10 − 5 = ____

4. 4 + 4 = ____

8 − 4 = ____

5. 8 + 8 = ____

16 − 8 = ____

6.
```
   7       14
 + 7     −  7
____     ____
```

7.
```
   3        6
 + 3     −  3
____     ____
```

8.
```
   9       18
 + 9     −  9
____     ____
```

Add.

Then find the differences.

9.
```
    5       12       12
 + 7     −  5     −  7
____     ____     ____
```

10.
```
    4       13       13
 + 9     −  4     −  9
____     ____     ____
```

11.
```
    6       16       16
 +10     −  6     − 10
____     ____     ____
```

12.
```
    7       15       15
 + 8     −  7     −  8
____     ____     ____
```

Subtract.

13.
```
  17
-  8
```

14.
```
  18
-  9
```

15.
```
  14
-  6
```

16.
```
  16
-  7
```

17.
```
  20
- 10
```

Write the missing numbers.

18. $12 - 6 =$ ____

$6 + $ ___ $= 12$

19. $17 - 8 =$ ____

$8 + $ ___ $= 17$

20. $16 - 9 =$ ____

$9 + $ ___ $= 16$

21. $13 - 8 =$ ____

$8 + $ ___ $= 13$

22. $15 - 9 =$ ____

$9 + $ ___ $= 15$

23. $13 - 4 =$ ____

$4 + $ ___ $= 13$

Complete the fact family.

24.

```
    7
+   8
_____
```

```
  +
_____
```

```
   15
-   7
_____
```

```
  -
_____
```

Problem Solving

Cross out information you do not need.
Solve.

Draw or write to explain.

25. Ryan finds **8** shells.
    Kaylee finds **9** shells.
    Oscar has **2** stones.
    How many shells do
    they find?

_____ shells

Adding Two-Digit Numbers

CHAPTER 21

INVESTIGATION

Add to find how many blue and red fish there are in all.

People Using Math

Norbert Wu

Norbert Wu is an underwater photographer. He takes pictures of plants and animals in the ocean. Some of the creatures he photographs are sharks, seals, and starfish. He takes pictures all over the world.

His pictures have been in many children's books. He has received many awards for his work.

Ben has a book of sea creatures. He finds **9** dolphins in one picture. **6** are in another picture. How many dolphins does he find?

Draw or write to explain.

_____ dolphins

Mental Math: Add Tens

When you add **tens,** think of an addition fact.

 3 + 5 = 8, so
30 + 50 = 80.

$3 + 5 = \underline{8}$

$3 \text{ tens} + 5 \text{ tens} = \underline{8} \text{ tens}$

$\underline{30} + \underline{50} = \underline{80}$

Guided Practice

Complete the addition sentences.

1.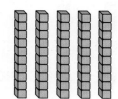

   Think
   I know
   4 + 4 = 8.

   $4 + 4 = \underline{}$

   $4 \text{ tens} + 4 \text{ tens} = \underline{} \text{ tens}$

   $\underline{} + \underline{} = \underline{}$

2.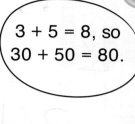

   $6 + 3 = \underline{}$

   $6 \text{ tens} + 3 \text{ tens} = \underline{} \text{ tens}$

   $\underline{} + \underline{} = \underline{}$

3. $4 + 1 = \underline{}$

   $4 \text{ tens} + 1 \text{ ten} = \underline{} \text{ tens}$

   $\underline{} + \underline{} = \underline{}$

4. $2 + 5 = \underline{}$

   $2 \text{ tens} + 5 \text{ tens} = \underline{} \text{ tens}$

   $\underline{} + \underline{} = \underline{}$

TEST TIPS **Explain Your Thinking** How does knowing $2 + 5 = 7$ help you solve $20 + 50$?

Remember to think of an addition fact when you add tens.

Complete the addition sentences.

1.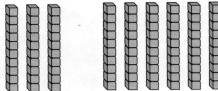

$3 + 6 = \underline{9}$

$3 \text{ tens} + 6 \text{ tens} = \underline{9} \text{ tens}$

$\underline{30} + \underline{60} = \underline{90}$

2.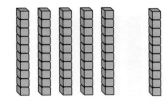

$5 + 1 = \underline{}$

$5 \text{ tens} + 1 \text{ ten} = \underline{} \text{ tens}$

$\underline{} + \underline{} = \underline{}$

3. $2 \text{ tens} + 1 \text{ ten} = \underline{} \text{ tens}$

$\underline{} + \underline{} = \underline{}$

4. $2 \text{ tens} + 3 \text{ tens} = \underline{} \text{ tens}$

$\underline{} + \underline{} = \underline{}$

5. $3 \text{ tens} + 4 \text{ tens} = \underline{} \text{ tens}$

$\underline{} + \underline{} = \underline{}$

6. $2 \text{ tens} + 2 \text{ tens} = \underline{} \text{ tens}$

$\underline{} + \underline{} = \underline{}$

7. $5 \text{ tens} + 3 \text{ tens} = \underline{} \text{ tens}$

$\underline{} + \underline{} = \underline{}$

8. $1 \text{ ten} + 8 \text{ tens} = \underline{} \text{ tens}$

$\underline{} + \underline{} = \underline{}$

Algebra Readiness ▶ Missing Addends

9. Deven has 30 stickers. He buys some more. Then he has 60 stickers. How many stickers does he buy?

Draw or write to explain.

_____ stickers

At Home Ask your child to explain how many tens are in the sum of 30 + 50.

Name_____

Two-Digit Addition Practice

Find $53 + 26$.

Step 1

Add the ones.

$$\begin{array}{r} 53 \\ +26 \\ \hline 9 \end{array}$$

Step 2

Add the tens.

$$\begin{array}{r} 53 \\ +26 \\ \hline 79 \end{array}$$

Guided Practice

Write the sum.

1. $\begin{array}{r} 80 \\ +12 \\ \hline \end{array}$

Think
Add the ones first.
Then add
8 tens + 1 ten.

2. $\begin{array}{r} 40 \\ +50 \\ \hline \end{array}$

3. $\begin{array}{r} 56 \\ +\ 2 \\ \hline \end{array}$

4. $\begin{array}{r} 70 \\ +\ 4 \\ \hline \end{array}$

5. $\begin{array}{r} 65 \\ +\ 3 \\ \hline \end{array}$

6. $\begin{array}{r} 20 \\ +\ 5 \\ \hline \end{array}$

7. $\begin{array}{r} 84 \\ +13 \\ \hline \end{array}$

8. $\begin{array}{r} 50 \\ +27 \\ \hline \end{array}$

9. $\begin{array}{r} 30 \\ +60 \\ \hline \end{array}$

10. $17 + 2 =$ ____

11. $85 + 3 =$ ____

12. $40 + 10 =$ ____

13. $10 + 80 =$ ____

14. $64 + 3 =$ ____

15. $20 + 20 =$ ____

TEST TIPS **Explain Your Thinking** How would you find the sum of
$20 + 20$ using mental math?

Write the sums.

Color the sums less than 50 ✏️ .

Color the sums greater than 50 ✏️ .

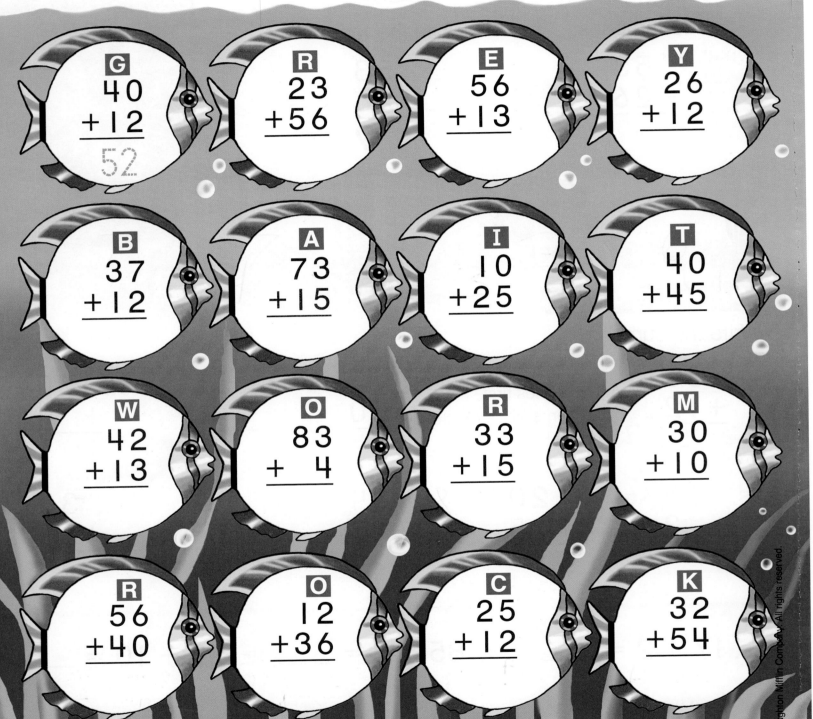

G
40
+12
52

R
23
+56

E
56
+13

Y
26
+12

B
37
+12

A
73
+15

I
10
+25

T
40
+45

W
42
+13

O
83
+ 4

R
33
+15

M
30
+10

R
56
+40

O
12
+36

C
25
+12

K
32
+54

Write the letters of the yellow fish in order.

___ ___ ___ ___ ___   ___ ___ ___ ___!

🏠 **At Home** Ask your child to write a two-digit addition problem that has a sum less than 50.

Name_____

Guess and Check

 MathTracks 2/30
Listen and Understand

Anya has money to buy
29 pompoms. She buys
two packs of pompoms.
Which two packs of
pompoms does Anya buy?

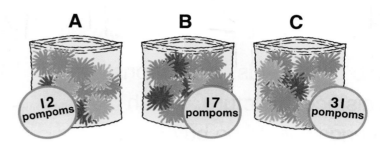

A B C

12 pompoms   17 pompoms   31 pompoms

UNDERSTAND

What do you know?

• Anya buys two packs of pompoms.
• Anya has money to buy **29** pompoms.

PLAN

Choose two different packs.

Try pack B and pack C.

How can you check your guess? _____add_____

SOLVE

Add to check.

pack B   17
pack C   +31
          48

*48 is too much.
Look for ones digits
that add to 9.*

pack A   12
pack B   +17
          29

Anya buys pack ___A___ and pack ___B___.

*The sum is 29. This is
the correct answer.*

LOOK BACK

Did you find the two packs Anya bought?
How do you know your answer makes sense?

Guided Practice

Remember:
► Understand
► Plan
► Solve
► Look Back

Use Guess and Check to solve.

These bags of buttons are for sale at the craft store.

A — 15 buttons
B — 21 buttons
C — 33 buttons
D — 44 buttons

1. Pablo only needs **59** buttons for his ocean picture. Which two bags should he buy?

Draw or write to explain.

Think
Find the ones digits with a sum of 9.

bag _____ and bag _____

2. Sandra needs **77** buttons. Which two bags should she buy?

Think
Look for numbers that make 77.

bag _____ and bag _____

Practice

3. Seti pours two bags of buttons into a box. He has **48** buttons in the box. Which two bags does he pour?

bag _____ and bag _____

4. Janet loses two bags of buttons. She loses **54** buttons. Which two bags does she lose?

bag _____ and bag _____

Go on

Name _____

Choose a Strategy

Solve.

1. Feathers come in bags of 8, 12, and 24. Corey needs 36 feathers for his penguin mask. Which two bags should he buy?

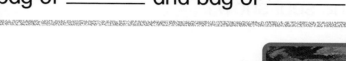 Draw or write to explain.

penguin

bag of _____ and bag of _____

2. Colleen has 20 dolphin pictures. Meg gives her 24 more. How many pictures does she have in all?

dolphin

_____ pictures

3. Paper squares are sold in boxes of 22, 34, and 75. Carlos only needs 97 squares for his coral reef picture. Which two boxes should he buy?

coral reef

box of _____ and box of _____

4. **Multistep** Fred has 31 seal stickers. His dad gives him 12 new stickers. Then his mom gives him 10 more. How many stickers does he have now?

seal

_____ stickers

 At Home Have your child gather groups of objects in your home and write a Guess and Check problem for you to solve.

Listen to your teacher read the problem.
Solve.

1. Mr. Akers brings his class of 26 children to the seal show. Ms. Char brings her class of 23 children. How many children do Mr. Akers and Ms. Char bring to the seal show?

Show your work using pictures, numbers, or words.

_____ children

2. Andrea has 18 tubes of paint. Lee has 31 tubes of paint. How many tubes of paint do Andrea and Lee have in all?

_____ tubes of paint

Listen to your teacher read the problem.
Choose the correct answer.

3. 38 sticks   35 sticks   25 sticks   22 sticks
        ○   ○   ○   ○

4. 36 feathers   27 feathers   26 feathers   16 feathers
        ○   ○   ○   ○

618 six hundred eighteen

Name_____

Vocabulary e · Glossary

Complete the sentence.

tens
ones

1. There are 6 _____ in the number 76.

2. There are 8 _____ in the number 86.

Concepts and Skills

Complete the addition sentences.

3.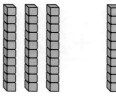

$3 + 2 =$ ____

3 tens + 2 tens = ____ tens

____ + ____ = ____

4.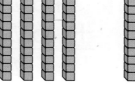

$4 + 4 =$ ____

4 tens + 4 tens = ____ tens

____ + ____ = ____

---

5. $1 + 5 =$ ____

1 ten + 5 tens = ____ tens

____ + ____ = ____

6. $6 + 3 =$ ____

6 tens + 3 tens = ____ tens

____ + ____ = ____

Use Workmat 5 with ▭▭▭ and ▫ .

Add. Write the sum.

7.
Tens	Ones
3	6
+	2

8.
Tens	Ones
2	4
+	5

9.
Tens	Ones
8	4
+	2

Chapter Review/Test

Use Workmat 5 with ▭▭▭▭▭▭ and ▭.
Add. Write the sum.

10.

Tens	Ones
6	1
+ 2	4

11.

Tens	Ones
7	5
+ 2	3

12.

Tens	Ones
4	2
+ 3	7

13.

Tens	Ones
1	4
+ 5	1

14.
$$\begin{array}{r} 30¢ \\ +59¢ \\ \hline ¢ \end{array}$$

15.
$$\begin{array}{r} 43¢ \\ + 6¢ \\ \hline ¢ \end{array}$$

16.
$$\begin{array}{r} 27¢ \\ +12¢ \\ \hline ¢ \end{array}$$

17.
$$\begin{array}{r} 56¢ \\ +22¢ \\ \hline ¢ \end{array}$$

18.
$$\begin{array}{r} 46 \\ + 0 \\ \hline \end{array}$$

19.
$$\begin{array}{r} 15 \\ +74 \\ \hline \end{array}$$

20.
$$\begin{array}{r} 30 \\ +35 \\ \hline \end{array}$$

21.
$$\begin{array}{r} 62 \\ + 6 \\ \hline \end{array}$$

22.
$$\begin{array}{r} 25 \\ +54 \\ \hline \end{array}$$

23. $35 + 54 =$ _____

24. $80 + 18 =$ _____

Problem Solving

Use Guess and Check to solve.

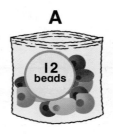

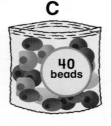

A — 12 beads
B — 32 beads
C — 40 beads

Draw or write to explain.

25. Min needs 52 beads to make necklaces for her family. Which two bags should she buy?

bag _____ and bag _____

Subtracting Two-Digit Numbers

CHAPTER 22

INVESTIGATION

How many more pins than patches are there?

Collect and Connect

Connect the dots.
Start at 50.
Finish at 100.

Name_____

Mental Math: Subtract Tens

When you subtract tens, think of a subtraction fact.

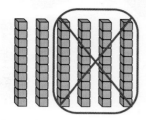

6 − 4 = 2, so
60 − 40 = 20.

Objective
Use basic facts and mental math to subtract tens.

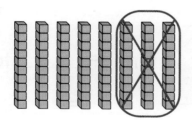

` − 4 = __2__

`tens − 4 tens = __2__ tens

`0 − 40 = 20

Guided Practice

omplete the subtraction sentences.

Think
I know
8 − 3 = 5.

8 − 3 = ____

8 tens − 3 tens = ____ tens

____ − ____ = ____

2.

7 − 4 = ____

7 tens − 4 tens = ____ tens

____ − ____ = ____

3. 9 − 5 = ____

9 tens − 5 tens = ____ tens

____ − ____ = ____

4. 9 − 3 = ____

9 tens − 3 tens = ____ tens

____ − ____ = ____

TEST TIPS **Explain Your Thinking** How does knowing 9 − 3 = 6
help you solve 90 − 30?

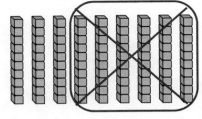

Complete the subtraction sentences.

1.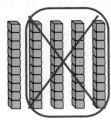

$9 - 6 =$ ___3___

9 tens $- 6$ tens $=$ ___3___ tens

___90___ $-$ ___60___ $=$ ___30___

2.

$5 - 4 =$ _____

5 tens $- 4$ tens $=$ _____ ten

_____ $-$ _____ $=$ _____

3. 6 tens $- 2$ tens $=$ _____ tens

_____ $-$ _____ $=$ _____

4. 7 tens $- 5$ tens $=$ _____ tens

_____ $-$ _____ $=$ _____

5. 9 tens $- 4$ tens $=$ _____ tens

_____ $-$ _____ $=$ _____

6. 8 tens $- 2$ tens $=$ _____ tens

_____ $-$ _____ $=$ _____

Problem Solving ▶ **Data Sense**

Use the bar graph to solve.

7. How many more cards than rocks does Jill have?

_____ more cards

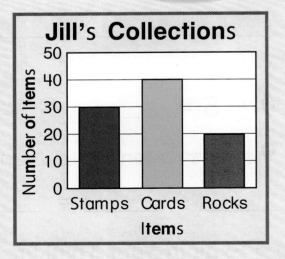

Jill's Collections

At Home Use the bar graph. Have your child write a subtraction sentence to find how many more stamps Jill has than rocks.

Subtract With Two-Digit Numbers

MathTracks 2/31
Listen and Understand

When subtracting from a two-digit number, subtract the ones first to find the **difference.**

Find **28 − 5.**

Objective
Subtract one-digit numbers from two-digit numbers.

Vocabulary
difference

Hands-On

Step 1
Show **28.**

Workmat 5	
Tens	**Ones**

Tens	Ones
2	8
−	5

Step 2
Subtract the ones.

Workmat 5	
Tens	**Ones**

Tens	Ones
2	8
−	5
	3

Step 3
Subtract the tens.

Workmat 5	
Tens	**Ones**

There are no tens to subtract.

Tens	Ones
2	8
−	5
2	3

Guided Practice

Use Workmat 5 with ▭▭▭▭▭ and ▱ .
Subtract. Write the difference.

1.

Tens	Ones
9	8
−	6

Think
First, subtract the ones.

2.

Tens	Ones
8	9
−	4

3.

Tens	Ones
5	9
−	2

TEST TIPS **Explain Your Thinking** How can you count back to find
59 − 2?

Remember to start subtracting with the ones.

Use Workmat 5 with ▭▭▭▭▭ and ◰.
Subtract. Write the difference.

1.

Tens	Ones
3	8
−	6
3	2

2.

Tens	Ones
2	8
−	2

3.

Tens	Ones
2	9
−	5

4.

Tens	Ones
3	9
−	4

5.

Tens	Ones
4	5
−	3

6.

Tens	Ones
5	6
−	2

7.

Tens	Ones
5	8
−	3

8.

Tens	Ones
6	9
−	3

9.

Tens	Ones
9	6
−	5

10.

Tens	Ones
7	6
−	4

11.

Tens	Ones
8	7
−	1

12.

Tens	Ones
8	7
−	5

Problem Solving ▷ Reasoning

13. The picnic ends at the time the clock shows. It starts 2 hours earlier. What time does the picnic start?

Draw or write to explain.

_____

14. Talk About It How did you find your answer?

At Home Have your child choose a few exercises from above. Ask him or her to explain how to find the difference.

Name_____

Subtract Two-Digit Numbers

MathTracks 2/32
Listen and Understand

Objective
Subtract two-digit numbers.

Find **36 − 14**.

Step 1

Show **36**.

Workmat 5

Tens	Ones

Tens	Ones
3	6
− 1	4

Step 2

Subtract the ones.

Workmat 5

Tens	Ones

Tens	Ones
3	6
− 1	4
	2

Step 3

Subtract the tens.

Workmat 5

Tens	Ones

Tens	Ones
3	6
− 1	4
2	2

Guided Practice

Use Workmat 5 with  and 🔲.
Subtract. Write the difference.

1.

Tens	Ones
8	9
− 5	6

Think
Subtract the ones.
Then subtract
8 tens − 5 tens.

2.

Tens	Ones
7	8
− 3	6

3.

Tens	Ones
5	6
− 2	4

TEST TIPS **Explain Your Thinking** How does knowing subtraction
facts help you subtract two-digit numbers faster?

First subtract the ones.
Then subtract the tens.

Use Workmat 5 with ▭▭▭▭▭▭▭ and ▱.
Subtract. Write the difference.

1.
Tens	Ones
5	8
− 3	5
2	3

2.
Tens	Ones
4	6
− 1	0

3.
Tens	Ones
3	8
− 1	6

4.
Tens	Ones
5	5
− 4	5

5.
Tens	Ones
7	0
− 2	0

6.
Tens	Ones
6	7
− 2	5

7.
Tens	Ones
8	9
− 4	6

8.
Tens	Ones
6	8
− 4	2

9.
Tens	Ones
8	4
− 3	2

10.
Tens	Ones
5	9
− 4	7

11.
Tens	Ones
9	6
− 5	5

12.
Tens	Ones
8	7
− 3	

13.
Tens	Ones
8	5
− 1	4

14.
Tens	Ones
9	7
− 4	2

15.
Tens	Ones
7	4
− 6	3

16.
Tens	Ones
9	5
− 6	3

Reading Math ▶ Vocabulary

17. Write a number sentence that shows
two numbers with a difference of thirty.

_____ ◯ _____ ◯ _____

At Home Ask your child to find 59 − 26. Have him or her explain the
steps used to solve the problem.

Name_____

Different Ways to Subtract

Objective
Use different ways to subtract.

There are different ways to subtract.

$$\begin{array}{r} 80 \\ -30 \\ \hline 50 \end{array}$$

I use
mental math.
8 − 3

$$\begin{array}{r} 57 \\ -25 \\ \hline 32 \end{array}$$

I use paper
and pencil.

$$\begin{array}{r} 65 \\ -20 \\ \hline 45 \end{array}$$

I use tens and
ones blocks.

Guided Practice

Choose a way to subtract.
Write the difference.

1.
Tens	Ones
5	6
−	2

Think
Count back to
find 56 − 2.

2.
Tens	Ones
9	8
− 6	8

3.
Tens	Ones
9	0
− 6	0

4.
Tens	Ones
8	5
− 4	2

5.
$$\begin{array}{r} 96 \\ -23 \\ \hline \end{array}$$

6.
$$\begin{array}{r} 60 \\ -40 \\ \hline \end{array}$$

7.
$$\begin{array}{r} 78 \\ -\ 3 \\ \hline \end{array}$$

8.
$$\begin{array}{r} 87 \\ -20 \\ \hline \end{array}$$

9.
$$\begin{array}{r} 56 \\ -\ 5 \\ \hline \end{array}$$

TEST TIPS **Explain Your Thinking** How did you find 56 − 5?

Choose a way to subtract.
Write the difference.

1.
Tens	Ones
5	6
− 2	5
3	

2.
Tens	Ones
7	0
− 4	0

3.
```
  98
-  3
____
```

4.
```
  76
- 24
____
```

5.
```
  59
-  9
____
```

6.
```
  67
- 35
____
```

7.
```
  46
- 20
____
```

8.
```
  80
- 30
____
```

9.
```
  45
- 13
____
```

10.
```
  97
- 63
____
```

11.
```
  75
-  2
____
```

12.
```
  50
- 10
____
```

13. 86 − 3 = _____

14. 58 − 2 = _____

15. 90 − 20 = _____

16. 50 − 40 = _____

17. 75 − 1 = _____

18. 60 − 40 = _____

Problem Solving ▷ Reasoning

19. **Multistep** Ana has 30 marbles in one box and 40 marbles in another box. She gives 10 marbles to Max. How many marbles does she have now?

Draw or write to explain.

_____ marbles

At Home Ask your child to subtract 75 − 35 and explain how he or she found the difference.

Go on ➡

Name _____

Now Try This Subtract Money Amounts

Subtract money the same way you subtract numbers.
Think of dimes and pennies as tens and ones.

Subtract.

Tens	Ones	
5	6	¢
− 2	2	¢
3	4	¢

Read **56¢** as **56 cents**.

56¢

Subtract.

1. 67¢
   −43¢
   24¢

2. 47¢
   − 5¢
   ¢

3. 68¢
   −21¢
   ¢

4. 40¢
   −10¢
   ¢

5. 44¢
   −10¢
   ¢

6. 38¢
   −16¢
   ¢

7. 89¢
   − 7¢
   ¢

8. 85¢
   −30¢
   ¢

9. 79¢
   −40¢
   ¢

10. 85¢
    −15¢
    ¢

11. 97¢
    −55¢
    ¢

12. 96¢
    −23¢
    ¢

Quick Check

Complete the subtraction sentences.

1. 7 tens − 3 tens = _____ tens

2. 9 tens − 6 tens = _____ tens

_____ − _____ = _____   _____ − _____ = _____

Use Workmat 5 with ▭▭▭▭▭▭▭▭▭ and ▭.
Subtract. Write the difference.

3.

Tens	Ones
2	9
−	1

4.

Tens	Ones
5	7
−	5

5.

Tens	Ones
7	3
− 6	2

6.

Tens	Ones
9	6
− 5	4

Social Studies
Connection

A Counting Board

Counting boards have been used for counting since ancient times.
They use beads to show place value.

The blue beads are in the ones place.
The red beads are in the tens place.

Write the number in different ways.

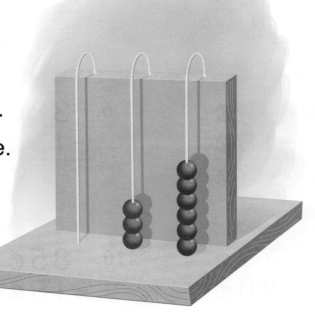

_____ tens _____ ones

_____ + _____ = _____

WEEKLY WR READER eduplace.com/kids/mw/

Two-Digit Subtraction Practice

Objective
Practice subtracting
two-digit numbers.

Find 86 − 25.

Step 1	**Step 2**
Subtract the ones.	Subtract the tens.
$\begin{array}{r}86 \\ -25 \\ \hline \end{array}$	$\begin{array}{r}86 \\ -25 \\ \hline 61 \end{array}$

Guided Practice

Write the difference.

1. $\begin{array}{r}47 \\ -35 \\ \hline \end{array}$ **Think** Subtract the ones first. Then subtract 4 tens − 3 tens.

2. $\begin{array}{r}68 \\ -5 \\ \hline \end{array}$

3. $\begin{array}{r}89 \\ -45 \\ \hline \end{array}$

4. $\begin{array}{r}35 \\ -4 \\ \hline \end{array}$

5. $\begin{array}{r}56 \\ -3 \\ \hline \end{array}$

6. $\begin{array}{r}87 \\ -13 \\ \hline \end{array}$

7. $\begin{array}{r}94 \\ -52 \\ \hline \end{array}$

8. $\begin{array}{r}75 \\ -2 \\ \hline \end{array}$

9. $\begin{array}{r}90 \\ -50 \\ \hline \end{array}$

10. 67 − 3 = ____

11. 80 − 50 = ____

12. 59 − 2 = ____

13. 50 − 40 = ____

14. 80 − 20 = ____

15. 73 − 3 = ____

TEST TIPS **Explain Your Thinking** How did you find the difference for 73 − 3?

Use a paper clip and a pencil.
Spin the spinner.
Write the number in the box. Subtract.

Spinner: 43, 5, 12, 31, 3, 24

59
− 43
16

76
− ☐
☐

85
− ☐
☐

96
− ☐
☐

87
− ☐
☐

56
− ☐
☐

75
− ☐
☐

69
− ☐
☐

77
− ☐
☐

65
− ☐
☐

97
− ☐
☐

58
− ☐
☐

86
− ☐
☐

79
− ☐
☐

89
− ☐
☐

 At Home Write the numbers 55, 65, 75, 85, and 95. Have your child spin the spinner. Then subtract the number on the spinner from the two-digit numbers.

Name _____

Check Subtraction

MathTracks 2/33
Listen and Understand

Add to check subtraction.

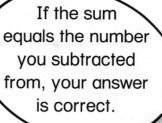

If the sum equals the number you subtracted from, your answer is correct.

Subtract.

$$\begin{array}{r} 48 \\ -36 \\ \hline 12 \end{array}$$

Check by adding.

$$\begin{array}{r} 12 \\ +36 \\ \hline 48 \end{array}$$

Guided Practice

Subtract. Check by adding.

Think
First find 57 − 24.
Then check by adding.

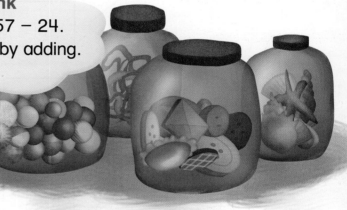

1.
$$\begin{array}{r} 57 \\ -24 \\ \hline 33 \end{array}$$

$$\begin{array}{r} 33 \\ +\ 24 \\ \hline 57 \end{array}$$

2.
$$\begin{array}{r} 98 \\ -64 \\ \hline \end{array}$$

+ ☐ / ☐ / ☐

3.
$$\begin{array}{r} 69 \\ -45 \\ \hline \end{array}$$

+ ☐ / ☐ / ☐

4.
$$\begin{array}{r} 76 \\ -\ 3 \\ \hline \end{array}$$

+ ☐ / ☐ / ☐

5.
$$\begin{array}{r} 80 \\ -60 \\ \hline \end{array}$$

+ ☐ / ☐ / ☐

TEST TIPS **Explain Your Thinking** How did you check $80 - 60$?

Practice

Add the difference and the number you subtracted.

Subtract. Check by adding.

1.
```
  64
-  2
  62
```
```
  62
+  2
  64
```

2.
```
  40
- 10
```
```
+
```

3.
```
  87
- 53
```
```
+
```

4.
```
  59
- 26
```
```
+
```

5.
```
  68
-  5
```
```
+
```

6.
```
  97
- 51
```
```
+
```

Problem Solving ▶ Data Sense

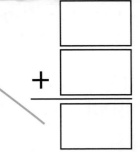

7. How many fewer red cars are there than green cars? _____

Model Cars	
Red	14
Blue	23
Green	35

8. **Write About It** Write a question you can solve by using the table.

_____

_____

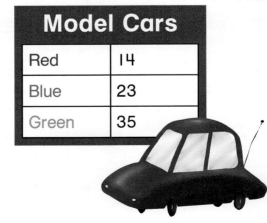

638 six hundred thirty-eight

At Home Ask your child to find 75 − 23. Then have him or her show you how to check the difference by adding.

Choose the Operation

Objective
Choose the correct operation to solve word problems.

Use addition to help you solve problems.

Polo collects marbles. He has 7 jars of black and white marbles. He has 12 jars of colored marbles. How many jars of marbles does he have?

Add to solve.

Think
I know both parts. I need to add to find the whole.

Whole	
19	
Part	**Part**
7	12

7 jars

+ 12 jars

_____

19 jars

_____19_____ jars of marbles

Use subtraction to help you solve problems.

Elena has 14 shells. 8 shells are white. The rest are brown. How many shells are brown?

Subtract to solve.

Think
I know the whole and one part. I need to subtract to find the missing part.

Whole	
14	
Part	**Part**
8	

☐ shells

○ ☐ white shells

_____

☐ brown shells

_____ shells are brown

Add or subtract to solve.

1. Jared finds **22** pennies. The next day he finds **14** pennies. How many pennies does Jared find?

Think
I need to find the total, so I add.

_____ pennies

2. Jason collects **29** gray rocks. He collects **13** white rocks. How many more rocks are gray than white?

Think
I need to compare the numbers, so I subtract.

_____ more rocks are gray

Practice

3. Kendi and Eric count **48** marbles on the table. **23** marbles roll away. How many marbles are left?

_____ marbles

4. Ellie has **16** paper clips. She collects **13** more paper clips. How many paper clips does Ellie have in all?

_____ paper clips

Go on ➡

Problem-Solving for Tests

Listening Skills

Listen to your teacher read the problem.
Solve.

1. Mrs. Rosen takes Henry to the park. He counts 48 leaves on the ground. 13 leaves blow away. How many leaves are left on the ground?

Show your work using pictures, numbers, or words.

_____ leaves

2. There are 8 buttons in the jar. The teacher puts 11 more buttons in the jar. How many buttons are in the jar now?

_____ buttons

Listen to your teacher read the problem.
Choose the correct answer.

3.　65 shells　　63 shells　　56 shells　　43 shells
　　　○　　　　　○　　　　　○　　　　　○

4.　8 chains　　10 chains　　11 chains　　18 chains
　　　○　　　　　○　　　　　○　　　　　○

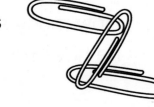

642 six hundred forty-two

Name _____

Solve.

1. Kendra has **20** acorns. She finds **9** more at the park. How many acorns does she have in all?

Draw or write to explain.

acorn

_____ acorns

2. There are **28** pine cones on the ground. **13** blow away. How many pine cones are on the ground?

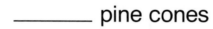

pine cone

_____ pine cones

3. **27** pebbles have stripes. **20** have spots. How many more pebbles have stripes than have spots?

pebbles

_____ pebbles

4. **Multistep** Jon finds **15** white shells and **10** black shells. He gives away **3** shells. How many shells does he have now?

shell

_____ shells

At Home Ask your child how he or she decided to solve each problem above.

Name _____

Write the difference.

1. 57
  − 25

2. 67
  − 5

3. 80
  − 30

4. 94
  − 52

5. 58 − 3 = _____

6. 40 − 20 = _____

Subtract. Check by adding.

7. 74
  − 2

☐
+ ☐
─────
☐

8. 60
  − 10

☐
+ ☐
─────
☐

9. 56
  − 21

☐
+ ☐
─────
☐

10. 97
   − 54

☐
+ ☐
─────
☐

Add or subtract to solve.

11. Pedro collects 8 rocks. Kelly collects 12 rocks. How many more rocks does Kelly collect than Pedro?

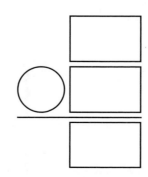

_____ more rocks

 **Key Topic Review**

Number the objects.
1 holds the least amount.
3 holds the greatest amount.

1.

———   ———   ———

Circle which holds more.

2. |

3.  |

Circle which can hold the same amount.

4. | |

---

5. |

 **Science Connection**

Weather

It is **90** degrees outside.
Circle what you would wear.

WEEKLY WR READER eduplace.com/kids/mw/

Chapter Review/Test

Vocabulary 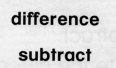 *e* Glossary

Complete the sentence.

> difference
>
> subtract

1. I _____ to find $38 - 5$.

2. The answer to a subtraction problem is the _____.

Concepts and Skills

Complete the subtraction sentences.

3.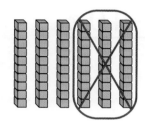

$6 - 3 =$ _____

6 tens $- 3$ tens $=$ _____ tens

_____ $-$ _____ $=$ _____

4.

$5 - 4 =$ _____

5 tens $- 4$ tens $=$ _____ ten

_____ $-$ _____ $=$ _____

5. 9 tens $- 2$ tens $=$ _____ tens

_____ $-$ _____ $=$ _____

6. 4 tens $- 2$ tens $=$ _____ tens

_____ $-$ _____ $=$ _____

Use Workmat 5 with ▭▭▭▭ and ▫ .
Subtract. Write the difference.

7.
Tens	Ones
3	7
−	5

8.
Tens	Ones
8	3
−	2

9.
Tens	Ones
5	9
− 2	8

10.
Tens	Ones
4	5
− 3	3

11. $48 - 5 =$ _____

12. $30 - 20 =$ _____

Subtract.
Write the difference.

13. 80 − 40 = _____

14. 82 − 10 = _____

15.
```
  85¢
− 53¢
─────
   ¢
```

16.
```
  18¢
−  7¢
─────
   ¢
```

17.
```
  70¢
− 40¢
─────
   ¢
```

Subtract.
Check by adding.

18.
```
  49
− 25
────
```
```
   ┌────┐
   │    │
   ├────┤
 + │    │
   ╞════╡
   │    │
   └────┘
```

19.
```
  60
− 30
────
```
```
   ┌────┐
   │    │
   ├────┤
 + │    │
   ╞════╡
   │    │
   └────┘
```

Problem Solving

Add or subtract to solve.

20. Zach finds 46 shells
at the beach. He gives
23 to Leah. How many
shells does he have left?

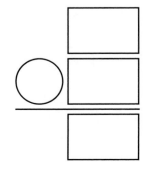

_____ shells

Name_____

Ishango Bone

Long ago, people in Africa used bones to help them count. This bone is one of the oldest bones used to count. It is called the Ishango Bone. It has marks on it that look like tally marks.

Look at the drawing of the African counting tool.

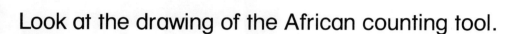

9   19   21   I I

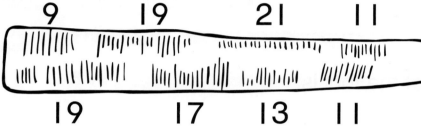

19   17   13   I I

Check your work by counting the marks on the bone.

Add or subtract to solve.   Draw or write to explain.

1. I I + I I = _____

2.   13
   +21
   ____

3.   19
   −17
   ____

4. 17 − 13 = _____

Today we write with pencils. The people who counted on the Ishango Bone did not have pencils. They made marks with a tool stored inside the top of the bone.

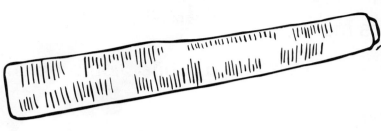

Solve the puzzle to learn what the tool is.
Add or subtract.

8 = K	32 = C	24 = A	38 = R	6 = O

$$\begin{array}{r} 13 \\ +11 \\ \hline \end{array} \qquad \begin{array}{r} 17 \\ +21 \\ \hline \end{array} \qquad \begin{array}{r} 17 \\ -11 \\ \hline \end{array} \qquad \begin{array}{r} 21 \\ +11 \\ \hline \end{array} \qquad \begin{array}{r} 19 \\ -11 \\ \hline \end{array}$$

____   ____   ____   ____   ____

⚙ Technology
Visit *Education Place* at
eduplace.com/kids/mw/
to learn more about this topic.

Vocabulary　(*e* • Glossary)

Match the word to the correct statement.

1. **difference**　　　　　a fact that adds the same two numbers

2. **double**　　　　　$100 = 10$ of these

3. **tens**　　　　　the answer to a subtraction problem

Concepts and Skills

Find the sum.

4. $\begin{array}{r} 7 \\ +7 \\ \hline \end{array}$　　5. $\begin{array}{r} 9 \\ +10 \\ \hline \end{array}$　　6. $\begin{array}{r} 4 \\ +5 \\ \hline \end{array}$　　7. $\begin{array}{r} 10 \\ +\ 3 \\ \hline \end{array}$　　8. $\begin{array}{r} 6 \\ +5 \\ \hline \end{array}$

9. $\begin{array}{r} 6 \\ 4 \\ +2 \\ \hline \end{array}$　　10. $\begin{array}{r} 2 \\ 9 \\ +1 \\ \hline \end{array}$　　11. $\begin{array}{r} 9 \\ 4 \\ +4 \\ \hline \end{array}$　　12. $\begin{array}{r} 7 \\ 3 \\ +2 \\ \hline \end{array}$　　13. $\begin{array}{r} 6 \\ 6 \\ +2 \\ \hline \end{array}$

Find the difference.

14. $\begin{array}{r} 16 \\ -\ 8 \\ \hline \end{array}$　　15. $\begin{array}{r} 18 \\ -\ 9 \\ \hline \end{array}$　　16. $\begin{array}{r} 14 \\ -10 \\ \hline \end{array}$　　17. $\begin{array}{r} 12 \\ -\ 9 \\ \hline \end{array}$　　18. $\begin{array}{r} 17 \\ -\ 8 \\ \hline \end{array}$

Complete the fact family.

19.
| 16 |
| 9 | 7 |

$\begin{array}{r} 9 \\ +7 \\ \hline \end{array}$　　$\begin{array}{r} \\ + \\ \hline \end{array}$　　$\begin{array}{r} 16 \\ -\ 9 \\ \hline \end{array}$　　$\begin{array}{r} \\ - \\ \hline \end{array}$

Unit 8 Test

Write the sum.

20.   45
      + 4

21.   21
      +56

22.   86
      +10

23.   50
      +49

Write the difference.

24.   80
      −50

25.   78
      −43

26.   26
      −14

27.   65
      −13

Subtract. Check by adding.

28.   76
      −31

+ ☐☐☐

29.   98
      −54

+ ☐☐☐

Problem Solving

Cross out information you do not need.
Solve.

30. There are 18 carrots in the garden. There are 9 tomatoes in the garden. 6 tomatoes are still green. How many more carrots than tomatoes are there?

Draw or write to explain.

_____ more carrots

1. Find 6 + 5 + 4.

Show your work using pictures, numbers, or words.

_____

2. Find 18 − 9.

Show your work using pictures, numbers, or words.

_____

Performance Assessment

Add or subtract to solve.
Write the number sentence.

3. Jack has 12 dimes in his bank.
He has 17 quarters in his bank.
How many coins does he have
in all?

quarter

dime

Show your work using pictures, numbers, or words.

_____ ◯ _____ ◯ _____

_____ coins

Estimate Sums

Use the number line to find the nearest ten.
Estimate the sum.

1.
$$\begin{array}{r} 43 \\ +31 \\ \hline \end{array}$$
nearest ten →
nearest ten →

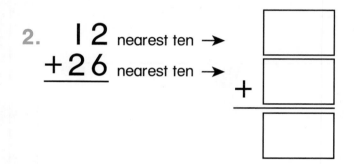

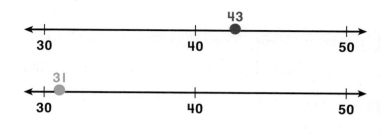

2.
$$\begin{array}{r} 12 \\ +26 \\ \hline \end{array}$$
nearest ten →
nearest ten →

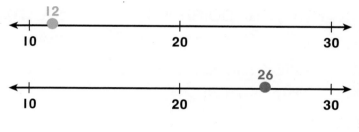

3.
$$\begin{array}{r} 38 \\ +48 \\ \hline \end{array}$$
nearest ten →
nearest ten →

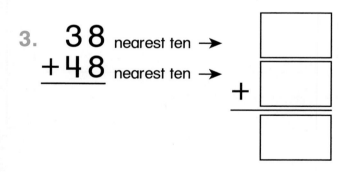

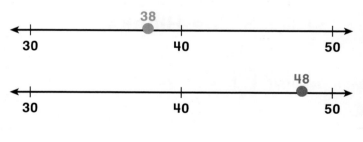

4.
$$\begin{array}{r} 71 \\ +86 \\ \hline \end{array}$$
nearest ten →
nearest ten →

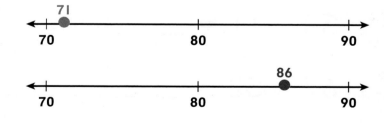

Technology
Visit *Education Place* at
eduplace.com/kids/mw/
for brain teasers.

Computer
Online Math

Use the Base Ten Blocks found at
eduplace.com/kids/mw/ to subtract.

Find 24 – 13.

1. Put your pointer over **Change Mat**.
   • Choose **Place Value**.

2. Put your pointer over the **Stamp** tool.
   • Click the **Ten Block** 2 times.
   • Click the **One Block** 4 times.
     This shows 24.

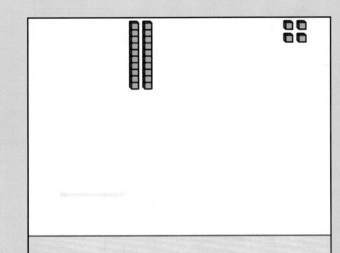

3. Use Erase to subtract.
   Click **Erase.**
   • Click the **Ten Block**.
   • Click 3 **One Blocks**.
     This subtracts 13.
   • Click [1 2 3].

Use Base Ten Blocks.
Find the difference.

1. 32 – 11 = _____

2. 48 – 6 = _____

3. 67 – 32 = _____

4. 55 – 23 = _____

5. 78 – 60 = _____

6. 94 – 64 = _____

Test-Taking Tips

· ·

Read each question at least twice.

Use what you know about numbers
to cut down on answer choices.

Multiple Choice

Fill in the ○ for the correct answer.

1.   4
   + 1 0

   6   8   12   14
   ○   ○   ○   ○

3.   6
     4
   + 7

   10   11   17   19
   ○   ○   ○   ○

2.   1 6
   −   8

   7   8   9   10
   ○   ○   ○   ○

4. Which one is a cylinder?

   ○   ○   ○   ○

Fill in the ○ for the correct answer.
N means Not Here.

Solve.

5. 42¢
   +37¢

   15¢   69¢   79¢   95¢
    ○   ○   ○   ○

6. Which container holds about
   1 quart?

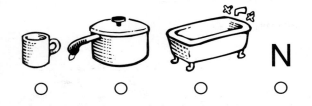
    ○   ○   ○   ○   N

7. 56
   −14

   31   52   60   N
    ○   ○   ○   ○

8. Cross out information you
   do not need.

   Roberto finds 12 clams.
   He gives 5 clams to Lee.
   Each clam has 2 shells.
   How many clams does
   Roberto have now?

   _____ clams

9. How much in all?

   _____ ¢

10. Mrs. Chang finds chopsticks
    in boxes of 8, 12, and 24.
    She only needs 32 chopsticks
    for a party. Which two boxes
    should she buy?   .

    box of _____

    and box of _____

 Test Prep on the Net
Visit *Education Place* at **eduplace.com/kids/mw/**
for more test prep practice.